The Business Cycle after Keynes

The Business Cycle after Keynes:

A Contemporary Analysis

A. W. Mullineux
Lecturer in Economics
University of Birmingham

BARNES & NOBLE BOOKS · NEW JERSEY

First published in Great Britain in 1984 by
WHEATSHEAF BOOKS LTD
A MEMBER OF THE HARVESTER PRESS PUBLISHING GROUP
Publisher: John Spiers
Director of Publications: Edward Elgar
16 Ship Street, Brighton, Sussex

and in the USA by
BARNES & NOBLE BOOKS
81 Adams Drive, Totowa, New Jersey 07516

British Library Cataloguing in Publication Data
Mullineux, A. W.
    The business cycle after Keynes
    1. Business cycle
    I. Title
    338.5'42   HB3711
ISBN 0-7108-0294-3

Library of Congress Cataloging in Publication Data
Mullineux, A. W.
    The business cycle after Keynes
    1. Business cycles.   2. Business cycles – Mathematical
models.   I. Title.
HB3714.M84   1984   338.5'42   83-27160
ISBN 0-389-20453-6

Typeset in 11 point Times by Radial Data Ltd, Bordon, Hants
Printed and bound in Great Britain by
Biddles Ltd, Guildford and King's Lynn

To Judith and Ruth

Contents

List of Figures

Preface

This book had its origins in the work done in preparation of my PhD thesis and a course of lectures which I presented to the final year economics undergraduates at the University of Birmingham in 1983. Its aim is to provide a text covering the multiplier–accelerator theory of the business cycle, usually discussed briefly in general macroeconomics textbooks, and the modern contributions to the business cycle literature pertaining to the political and equilibrium theories of the business cycle. In this latter respect it covers important material which is not readily available in undergraduate textbooks. In addition the roles of the government, the linearity assumption and nonlinearity, in business cycle modelling, are discussed. It is hoped that the renewed interest in business cycle theory will filter through to the undergraduate macroeconomic course level and that this book will provide a useful supplement to macroeconomic textbooks in the manner that short texts on growth theory have done in the past.

As the title implies, the book concentrates on contributions to business cycle theory made after the publication of Keynes's *General Theory* in 1936. The reasons for this are twofold. First, the aim is to provide a short supplementary textbook on modern business cycle theory rather than an all encompassing treatise on business cycle theory. By elaborating on the multiplier–accelerator model and discussing the modern theories of the cycle in some depth, it is my view that a fairly balanced view of the major issues in business cycle theory can be gleaned. This is because many of the issues raised in the older debates have re-arisen in the modern business cycle literature. Secondly, major works already exist which survey, in detail, pre-Keynesian contributions to the business cycle literature, e.g. A. Hansen (1964), *Business Cycles and National Income* and G. Haberler (1958), *Prosperity and Depression.* The literature on the Marxist (Marxian) theories of the cycle is also ignored in this short text, due to the existence of good surveys elsewhere – see references in the text. It is to be stressed that the subject of this book is business cycle theory, rather than economic cycle theory in general. The business cycle is usually taken to have a duration of approximately 40-60 months; longer cycles are only briefly discussed, although references to some of the literature are provided in the text.

The book is written to a level which should be within the reach of second or third year students who have done introductory economics, and mathematics and statistics courses. For those in need of a brief refresher on differential and difference equations an Appendix is provided.

I would like to acknowledge my debt to Marilyn Mansell, who typed the first draft quickly and efficiently, despite my atrocious handwriting and spelling, and my wife Judith, for suffering my hours of preoccupation whilst I prepared the original manuscript.

1 An Introduction to Business Cycle Analysis and Modelling

1.1 INTRODUCTION

In this chapter a number of concepts and definitions concerning the business cycle will be introduced. The chapter is organised as follows: Section 1.2 describes the main features of business, or trade, cycles; Section 1.3 discusses the period of business cycles; Section 1.4 considers the question of the existence of business cycles; and, finally, Section 1.5 discusses the sort of model that is appropriate for explaining the generation of business cycles.

1.2 WHAT IS THE BUSINESS CYCLE?

There are many definitions of the economic phenomenon called the business or, synonymously, the trade cycle. The problem is that the majority of these definitions implicitly, or explicitly, suggest a cause of the phenomenon to be explained. A similar problem arises in the definition of inflation, in which case the most appropriate solution seems to be to adopt a definition that amounts to describing the statistical series to be explained by inflation theory, namely the rate of increase of the price level. The statistical phenomena to be explained, in the case of the business cycle, are the serial correlation in the deviation of output from trend and the serial correlation in a number of other economic series which exhibit co-movements, be they pro- or anti-cyclical and with or without a lag, with output. Taking the above description of the statistical phenomena to be explained as our working definition of the business cycle, then business cycle theory addresses itself to explaining these statistical phenomena.

Evidence concerning the existence of business cycles can be found in the economic time series of most, if not all, industrial countries. The problem of explaining the business cycle taxed economists even before detailed collection of economic data became widespread and there is every indication that the business cycle is at least as old as the capitalist economic system itself. There is some debate about whether centrally planned economies would be free of business cycle, if it were not for their interaction with the capitalist (mixed) economies of the West, and whether the cycle is less pronounced in these countries (see Bronfenbrenner (ed.) (1969) for further discussion). As Mathews (1959) points out, roughly the same path is followed by all the chief indices of the state of prosperity in the economy, e.g. production, national income, employment, profits, etc. In addition, he notes that some series are more volatile than others and that they are not all subject to the same upward trend. For example, investment shows more volatility than consumption, and unemployment has not followed the same trend as output. A complete theory of the cycle must not only explain the movement of one of the indicators of prosperity, such as national income, over time but must also explain the co-movements of other important economic time series.

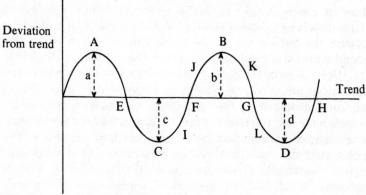

Figure 1.1: Features of the business cycle

The deviations of output, and other variables, from trend have a structure as depicted in Figure 1.1. They typically follow an expansionary phase, to a peak (A), succeeded by a contractionary phase, to a trough (C), followed by another expansion to the next peak (B) and so on.

The terms 'boom' and 'slump' are also commonly used in connection with the business cycle, but the usage of these terms is often not clear. We shall take them to have the following meanings: The boom is the period of rapid expansion, I–J for example, succeeding a period of tentative recovery and before a slowdown in growth occurs, perhaps due to 'bottlenecks' in various sectors of the economy. The slump is the period of rapid contraction, K—L for example, in which it is clear that the peak has been passed and that a recession in economic activity is imminent, to the point where the rate of decline begins to decrease and the recession is said to be 'bottoming out'.

The contractionary phase is sometimes called a recession or a depression; but in the more recent literature these two terms have taken on different meanings. The former is used to describe a slowdown in growth, such that the growth rate becomes less than the trend growth rate, and is part of a growth cycle. The latter term was coined to describe the cycles experienced in the 1950s and 1960s, when the cycle appeared to consist of alternating speeds of growth and in which no real decline in output occurred. The term depression is reserved for contractions that result in a fall in real output, rather than periods of relatively slow growth. Two collections of articles, edited by Zarnowitz (1972) and Bronfenbrenner (1969), came to the conclusion that depressions were a thing of the past, because the business cycle had changed in nature since the second world war, and had become a growth cycle. Since the late 1960s a number of major economies have experienced depressions and we have, therefore, seen a return to the more traditional business, as opposed to growth, cycle. A number of theories have been offered to explain this experience, including: those based on the emergence of newly-industrialised economies to challenge the traditional industrial powers of the advanced western economies; those based on the increase in world economic interdependence; and those based on the effects of the OPEC oil price shocks of 1973 and 1979. An alternative explanation, subscribed to by Mandel (1980) amongst others, is that the 1950s and 1960s marked a period in which business cycles evolved around an upward trend which was in fact the upswing of a long wave, with duration roughly in accordance with that postulated by Kondratieff (1935), namely, 50–60 years. Similarly, in the 1970s and 1980s, we are experiencing business cycles around the downswing of the wave. Whether this means that we are in for a period of zero or negative growth largely depends on whether the long wave itself has a zero or a positive growth trend.

Business cycles, and cycles in general, are usually described by a number of features, such as period, amplitude and degree of dampening. The period of a cycle is the length of time necessary for the completion of a full cycle and may be measured in a number of alternative ways: (1) time between successive peaks, e.g. A and B; (2) time between successive troughs, e.g. C and D; (3) time between successive upcrosses (of a trend), e.g. F and H; and (4) time between successive downcrosses, e.g. E and G. These alternative measures of period will only be equivalent if the cycle is very regular, following a sine wave for example. The amplitude of the cycle is, essentially, a measure of the severity of the cycle. It may be measured by the total difference of successive peaks and troughs from the trend, e.g. a+c or c+b or b+d. The dampening factor describes the extent to which the cycle maintains energy. A cycle with a dampening factor of zero repeats itself forever, conserving all the energy that generated it, e.g. a sine curve. Such cycles are called conservative cycles. A cycle with a positive dampening factor is one in which energy is dissipated so that the cycle will gradually die out and demonstrate a declining amplitude, and perhaps period, over time, as depicted in Figure 1.2a. Finally, a cycle with a negative dampening factor has an increasing amplitude, and perhaps period, see Figure 1.2b.

The actual statistical series to be explained by business cycle theory do not correspond to any of the cases depicted in Figures 1.1 and 1.2. Instead, the series show an expansion phase which is longer than the contraction phase, at least in most of the post-second world war period prior to 1973, and in which there seems to be a rather erratic movement around the basic cycle

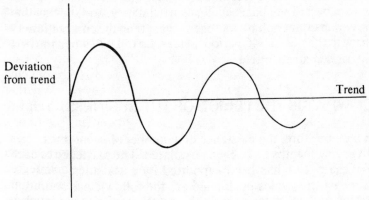

Deviation from trend

Trend

Figure 1.2a Positive dampening

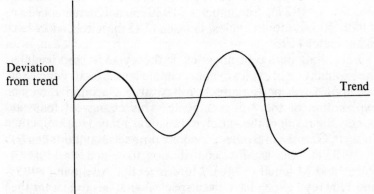

Deviation from trend

Trend

Figure 1.2b: Negative dampening

around the trend. This latter feature is due in part to seasonal influences and is only really discernible when quarterly or monthly observations are available. Time series, for real income in the US and the UK for example, do not in fact show clearly defined regular cycles. The cycles would be more clearly marked if detrended series were graphed and if longer series of quarterly or monthly, rather than annual, data were available. The problem is that it is not clear whether the same trend applied throughout the period, especially in the pre-and post-1973 periods, or which method of detrending is appropriate.

Thus business cycle theory must address itself to the explanation of the basic cycle, its irregularity, and the fact that the expansionary phase has been longer than the contractionary phase in the post-1946 period, at least up to 1974 when the first oil crisis had its effect.

1.3 WHAT IS THE PERIOD OF THE BUSINESS CYCLE?

In the literature, the existence of a number of economic cycles of varying lengths have been postulated. The existence of each of these cycles has been supported by a statistical analysis. Amongst the cycles postulated are the following: Kondratieff (1935), 50-60 year waves; Kuznets, 15-25, year cycles, Kuznets (1930), Lewis and O'Leary (1955), Isard (1942); major, 6-10, year cycles, Hansen (1951), Juglar (1889), Wardwell (1927), Schumpeter (1939) and Kitchen (1923); minor, 40-60, month cycles, Hansen (1951), Kitchen (1923), Schumpeter (1939).

For a long period business cycle theory addressed itself to the explanation of cycles of approximate length 6–10 years, but in the post-war period attention has turned, primarily, to the explanation of the 3-5 year cycle. This change of focus is largely the result of the massive statistical analysis of US, UK, French, German and other economic time series undertaken by the NBER,[1] the seminal contribution to which was that of Burns and Mitchell (1946). More recently, Adelman (1965) and Howrey (1968) have used spectral analysis to test for the existence of cycles with a period longer than 40-60 months. They find little supportive evidence for the long swing hypothesis of cycles of duration longer than fifteen years, but Howrey finds some support for the existence of major cycles.

In spite of the findings of Howrey and Adelman, interest in long waves has persisted, with Mandel (1980) being perhaps the most persuasive advocate of their existence. It should be observed that the possibility of proving exclusively the existence, or otherwise, of long waves using standard statistical techniques is severely restricted by the length of reliable economic time series. Most reliable series encompass, at most, two or three of the postulated Kondratieff (1935) waves. The long waves discussed by Mandel have erratic periods, but broadly fall into the 40-60 year range. They are thus of about the same length as the fluctuations postulated by Kondratieff (1935). Mandel, however, differentiates between the long cycles postulated by Kondratieff, and the long waves postulated by the Marxist theory of capitalist development. Kondratieff's cycles were regarded as being repeated fluctuations caused by endogenous factors, such as shifting terms of trade. In contrast Mandel's long waves are initiated by a major exogenous shock, such as a technological revolution. Once initiated the expansion follows an endogenously determined path which leads, inevitably, to a contraction, which continues until some other shock hits the system. This shock could be another positive exogenous stimulus to capitalism or a workers' revolution bringing about its demise.

1.4 DOES THE BUSINESS CYCLE EXIST?

McCulloch (1975, 1977), Savin (1977) and Anderson (1977) have questioned the very existence of the business cycle. They argue that economic time series are so irregular that no regular cycle is discernible and that the deviations from trend represent uncorrelated responses to random events, in which case no theory is required to explain the cycle at all.

Ranged against these findings are the impressive statistical analyses undertaken by the NBER of cycles in the major economic series and their co-movements. In addition, we have the results of the spectral analysis, undertaken by Howrey (1968), which indicate that a 40-60 month cycle exists; and the stylised business cycle facts, listed in Lucas (1977) and Sargent (1979). The methods used by the NBER to date post-war business cycles are described in Mintz (1969).

Given the statistical complexity of the debates involving the existence of business, and also longer, cycles, we cannot pursue these matters here. We shall instead adopt the prevalent view that 40-60 month business cycles are sufficiently evident, in the deviations of economic variables from their trends, to warrant explanation. We shall have to reserve judgement on the existence of longer cyles or waves and assume that they can be explained independently of the business cycle.

1.5 WHAT SORT OF MODEL SHOULD BE USED TO EXPLAIN BUSINESS CYCLES?

There are basically two alternative ways of modelling the cycle, linearly and nonlinearly. The former approach employs only linear equations to explain the cycle, and the latter utilises nonlinear equations. Each of these two types of model may be analysed deterministically (without shocks) or stochastically (with shocks). We shall look at examples of applications of these various modelling procedures, and their implications, in the next two chapters.

Chapter 2 will discuss business cycle modelling in the period following the publication of Keynes's *General Theory* in 1936, to 1975, when two major new contributions to business cycle theory and modelling were made. Chapter 3 will discuss business cycle theory and modelling in the post-1975 period.

Before moving on, a discussion of the contributions of Frisch (1933) and Slutsky (1927) to business cycle modelling is germane. Slutsky observed that random statistical series could be converted into cyclical series, by taking a moving average of the random series. The moving average equation thus acted as a frequency converter, in that it transformed a random series into a cyclical series. Frisch developed this idea within the context of business cycle analysis, suggesting that the explanation of the business cycle required the solution to two problems: the 'propagation problem' and the 'impulse problem'. The solution to the impulse problem would be a shock-generating model and the solution to the propagation model would be an economic model capable of converting the shocks, emanating from the shock-generating model, into a business cycle conforming to statistical observations. Frisch initially considered linear models with random shocks, using differential equations with damped cyclical solutions.[2] Also, implicit in the work of Slutsky, there is the possibility of using difference equations, with monotonically damped solutions,[3] and an impulse model capable of generating serially correlated shocks. The Frisch–Slutsky analysis showed, therefore, that linear stochastic models were capable of generating cycles if the econmy is stable, i.e. if the solution to the propagation model is damped, so that, in the absence of shocks, the economy would naturally grow along the trend line. Explanation of the trend in economic development could then be confined to a fully separable growth theory. The role of anti-cyclical policy, in this scenario, was to try to offset the effects of the shocks by alleviating booms and slumps. The government was to undertake such counter-cyclical policy on behalf of the public, in order to minimise the negative welfare effects of the cycle.

The Slutsky—Frisch modelling procedure of utilising a stable linear stochastic model to explain the cycle was welcomed by econometricians who became increasingly adept at using linear techniques in the post-war period. This approach to business cycle modelling was adopted by most Keynesians and it has also been utilised by the new classical economists, see for example Lucas and Sargent (1978).

2 Business Cycle Modelling: 1936–1975

2.1 INTRODUCTION

This chapter considers various contributions to the business cycle literature made in the period between the publication of Keynes's *General Theory* in 1936, and the publication of two important contributions to business cycle theory, in 1975, which will be discussed in the next chapter.

The chapter is organised as follows: Section 2.2 introduces linear deterministic business cycle modelling in the context of the multiplier–accelerator model; Section 2.3 examines the mathematical solution to linear deterministic equations; Section 2.4 examines the possible stochastic solutions to linear equations; Section 2.5 discusses a number of nonlinear business cycle models; Section 2.6 discusses the limitations of the linearity assumption; Section 2.7 considers the role of the government in the business cycle; Section 2.8 discusses the monetary theory of the cycle; and, finally, Section 2.9 provides a summary and some conclusions.

2.2 THE LINEAR, DETERMINISTIC, MULTIPLIER–ACCELERATOR MODEL

Samuelson (1939) developed a linear multiplier—accelerator model[1] which may be stated as follows:

$$Y_t = g_t + C_t + I_t \qquad \qquad 2.1$$
$$C_t = \alpha Y_{t-1} \qquad \qquad 2.2$$

$$I_t = \beta \, |C_t - C_{t-1}| \qquad\qquad 2.4$$
$$g_t = 1$$

where Y_t is national income, g_t is government expenditure, C_t is

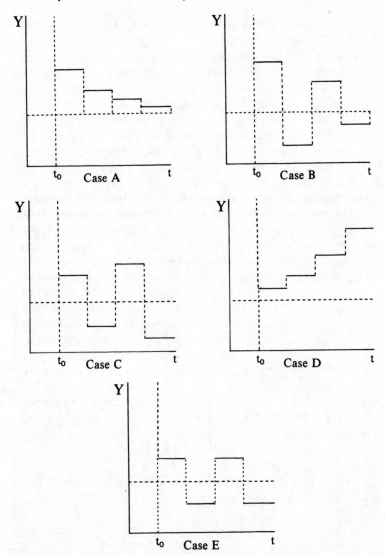

Figure 2.1: Solution paths to the linear deterministic multiplier–accelerator model

consumption expenditure, and I_t is induced private investment, all at time t. These equations reduce to a second order linear difference equation in output, i.e.

$$Y_t = 1 + \alpha\,[1 + \beta]\,Y_{t-1} - \alpha\beta Y_{t-2} \qquad\qquad 2.5$$

Samuelson demonstrated that there are various solution paths for national income to be derived from this model, depending on the values of the roots of the equation 2.5 or, equivalently, the relationships between the parameters α and β.[2]

In general, a number of solution paths for a second order linear difference equation are possible. The various possible responses to a positive, unsustained, displacement to g_t at time t_0 are shown in Figure 2.1. The relationships between the parameter values, in this specific example, necessary to give these various solution paths are shown in Figure 2.2. Negative displacements result in similar solution paths, but with income starting below the original equilibrium following the shock so that, in case D, income will decrease at an increasing rate. Sustained displacements to government expenditure will yield similar solution paths except that the respective solution paths

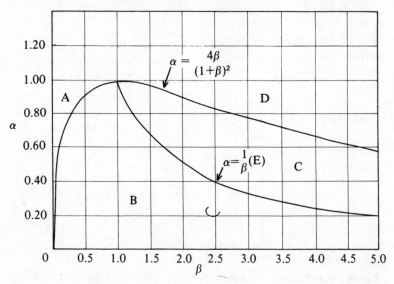

Figure 2.2: The parameter relationships which yield the various solution paths to the multiplier–accelerator model

will converge to, diverge from, or oscillate around, a new asymptotic equilibrium which is $(1/1-\alpha)$ times the constant level of government expenditure, see Samuelson (1939). Finally, in case B, perfectly regular periodic fluctuations in g_t will result eventually in fluctuations of income of the same period.

2.3 SOLUTIONS TO SECOND ORDER LINEAR DETERMINISTIC EQUATIONS[3]

More generally, a second order linear homogeneous difference equation, with a complex conjugate pair of roots, will give: a conservative cycle around the equilibrium, if D=1 (e.g. Case E, Figure 2.1); a damped cycle, if D<1 (e.g. Case B, Figure 2.1); or an explosive cycle, if D>1 (e.g. Case C, Figure 2.1); where D is the square root of the imaginary root squared, i.e. the square root of the sum real part of the imaginary root squared and the complex part squared. In this imaginary roots case the phase[4] and the amplitude of the cycle will depend on the initial conditions.

Apart from cases where imaginary roots occur, negative roots will also result in cycles in linear difference equations. In the first order case a root of minus one gives a regular cycle, roots lying between minus one and zero yield damped cycles, and negative roots, greater than one in absolute value, give explosive oscillations. The period of these cycles is two, but the phase and the amplitude depend on the initial conditions.

Linear differential equations, of order greater than one, only offer the possibility of cycles if imaginary roots occur. Since these occur in complex conjugate pairs, it is to be noted that first order differential equations cannot yield cycles, and that equations of order n, where n is odd, must have at least one real root. The cycles resulting in the imaginary roots case may be either explosive, damped or constant in amplitude and period.

In the second order homogeneous case in which the two roots form a complex conjugate pair: if the real part of these roots is zero, conservative oscillations occur; if the real part is less than zero, damped cycles result; and, finally, explosive cycles occur if the real part is greater than zero. In nth order (n>2) equations, in which both real and imaginary roots occur and where there may be more than one pair of imaginary roots, dynamic behaviour is dominated by the root with the largest real part.[5] Slight complications arise in the cases of repeated real roots or pairs of imaginary roots, which provide the possibility, even in the homogeneous case, of cycles around a moving equilibrium rather than a constant. Any cycles produced by linear differential equations will be dependent on the initial conditions which determine the amplitude and phase of the cycle.

In the nth order ($n > 2$) linear difference equation case, with imaginary roots, repeated roots introduce the possibility of cycles around a moving equilibrium, rather than a constant, and the dominant root determines the long-run dynamic behaviour.[6] Again the cycles produced will be dependent on the initial conditions. In the $n > 1$ case negative roots will also lead to oscillations even if they are not dominant.

For both the difference and differential equation cases, the particular solution may differ from the solution to the homogeneous equation, with the result that a moving equilibrium may replace a constant equilibrium (at zero) ensured by the homogeneous solution, even in the absence of repeated real roots or repeated pairs of complex roots.

There are a number of useful texts which analyse applications of difference and differential equations to cycle theory. The major works are Allen (1965), Baumol (1959) and Gandolfo (1980), the last having a very wide coverage, although most mathematical economics textbooks have at least some examples. A commonly-used text on difference equations is Goldberg (1961), and a major reference on differential equations is Coddington and Levinson (1955), although most good textbooks on mathematics for economists deal with difference and differential equations to an adequate level.

It will be instructive next to consider the usefulness of the various types of solution path depicted in Figure 2.1, or their continuous time equivalents, for business cycle analysis and modelling.

2.4 SOLUTIONS TO SECOND ORDER LINEAR STOCHASTIC EQUATIONS[7]

The least likely solution to the second order linear deterministic model, in terms of the probability of the required parameter relationship occurring, is the conservative oscillation case (case E). This, however, might look the most promising solution from the cycle modelling point of view. But, as soon as the existence of shocks, and the necessity for stochastic modelling, is admitted, this solution loses its usefulness. This is because the cycle involved conserves all energy and hence the shocks, by imparting extra energy, lead to an increase in the amplitude of the cycle as they accrue. This is demonstrated numerically by Klein and Preston (1969) in their analysis of the linear conservative Dresche (1947) model. Thus within a stochastic environment, case E is of little use, unless the explosiveness of the cyle can somehow be contained.

The same essentially applied to cases C and D, i.e. the explosive cyclical and monotonically explosive cases, since the additional energy imparted by the shocks, in case C, will certainly not attenuate the cycle and may even aggravate it, and, in case D, they may actually impart some randomness.

The monotonically and cyclically convergent cases, A and B, do, however, become interesting in a linear stochastic framework. Random shocks hitting the cyclically convergent case may, if they are of sufficient size, offset the positive dampening. In the case of monotonic dampening, negatively serially correlated shocks may be required to generate a cycle. These convergent cases, and their continuous time equivalents, thus form a useful basis for linear stochastic cycle modelling. Frisch (1933), as we noted in the previous chapter, analysed the case which a cyclical convergent deterministic (propagation) model with random shocks, from an impulse model, imposed. Keynesian econometric models of the 1960s and early 1970s were found to possess monotonically convergent solutions (see Adelman and Adelman, 1959; Hickman (ed.), 1972). Stochastic simulations with these models required serially correlated shock generating processes to track the business cycle. These Keynesian econometric models also include, in addition to multiplier—accelerator interaction, inventory investment as a channel imparting cyclical influence. Metzler's (1941) model, which yields a second order difference equation in inventories, is a good example of an inventory cycle model.

A final point of interest regarding linear stochastic, or linear deterministic, models with explosive solutions is that these too could be used to generate a business cycle if the explosiveness could somehow be contained, by a ceiling and a floor on the economy. This leads us on to the consideration of nonlinear business cycle modelling.

With regard to stochastic linear difference equations, a major reference is Mann and Wald (1943), although economists have become increasingly familar with such equations through times series analysis, which uses autoregressive-moving average models (see Box and Jenkins, 1971). Also, concerning the role of the accelerator and multiplier—accelerator interaction in the cycle in stochastic models, see Chow (1968) and Chow and Levitan (1969 a and b).

2.5 NONLINEAR BUSINESS CYCLE MODELLING

Hicks (1949), in his discussion of Harrod's (1948) growth theory, observed that the explosive solution to linear deterministic second order difference or differential equations could be employed for cycle analysis. What was required was a ceiling and a floor, in order to contain the explosiveness, so that national income was constrained between these limits to the economic possibilities. Hicks used the monotonic explosive solution in his model, but it is clear that the cyclically explosive solution or stochastically explosive models would have served equally well; these alternatives would have allowed more variability in the period and amplitude of the resulting cycle.

In Hicks's model, which is developed further in Hicks (1950), the ceiling and floor grew at the same, exogenously given rate (g) as the trend. The resulting cycle is depicted in Figure 2.3, and may be described as follows. A positive shock will take the economy away from equilibrium growth, to B, via the multiplier—accelerator interaction. Once the ceiling is reached, at B, the rate of increase of output is slowed up, and induced investment is reduced to that corresponding to the rate

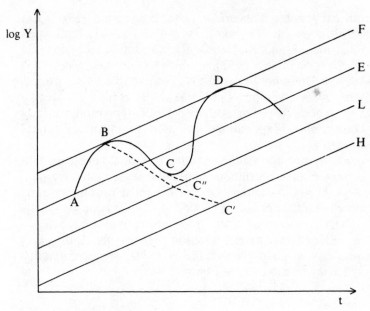

Figure 2.3: Hicks's trade cycle

Notes: F = full employment ceiling
E = upper equilibrium
L = lower equilibrium
H = long-range investment

of growth of output (g), along the ceiling (F). This rate of induced investment is only sufficient to engender a level of output that approximates to the line E. Output therefore tends to move back towards E, along B − C' and would continue to fall along this line if the accelerator operated in a downward direction. Dropping the accelerator (i.e. setting induced investment equal to zero) for the downward path, so that only the multiplier operates, takes the economy along B—C". Since L is upward sloping B—C" will have begun to turn up at C and the accelerator comes back into action, leading to positive induced investment, and causing the path to diverge from C—C". Expansion takes the economy through E to D, and the cycle is complete and self-perpetuating.

Thus Hicks was able to generate a cycle from the mono-tonically explosive solution to the mutliplier-accelerator model by imposing, in the form of a ceiling and a floor to the economy and an irreversible accelerator, what Samuelson (1947) has called 'billiard table nonlinearities' and what we shall call type I nonlinearities. Gandolfo (1980) gives a useful discussion of a model due to Smithies (1957), in which a multiplier–accelerator model with type I nonlinearities is used to explain both growth and the cycle. Another similar example is due to Minsky (1959). In both cases Duesenberry (1949)-type ratchet effects on consumption expenditure are used to introduce type I nonlinearities.

An alternative approach to nonlinear business cycle modelling is to introduce continuous nonlinearities, or what we shall call type II nonlinearities. One of the most prominent early examples of this approach is Goodwin's (1951) analysis of the multiplier–accelerator model. The nonlinearity introduced was in the induced investment function (see Figure 2.4b). This function may be compared with the induced investment function used in Hicks's model (see Figure 2.4a).

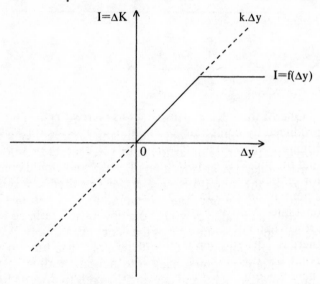

Figure 2.4a: Hicks's investment function (accelerator)

Notes:
$\Delta K = I$ = induced investment
Δy = change in output
k = acceleration coefficient

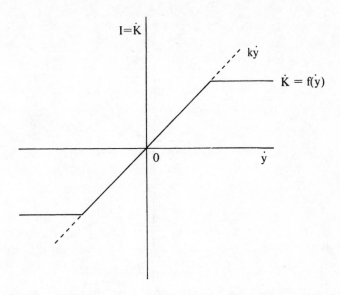

Figure 2.4b: Goodwin's investment function (accelerator)

Notes:
$\dot{K} = I$ = induced investment
$\dot{y}$ = growth in output
k = acceleration coefficient

One of the cycles discussed in Goodwin's (1951) paper is produced by combining the nonlinear accelerator, depicted in Figure 2.4b, with a dynamical multiplier, to allow for the fact that the process of multiplication takes time. The solution path for output (y) is depicted, on the phase plane, in Figure 2.5. There is an equilibrium point, E, at the origin, but this is unstable. A positive shock would, therefore, lead to explosive growth to point A. At A the development becomes untenable and there is a discontinuous change in $\dot{y}$, the time derivative of y, to point B. Output then grows until C is reached, at which point there is a jump to D followed by a contraction to A, and so forth. There is, therefore, a closed path A,B,C,D, constituting a self-sustaining cycle in output (y). The discontinuities should be considered as an approximation to a rapid change. Goodwin discusses a number of models, based on nonlinear investment functions, and demonstrates their potential to generate limit

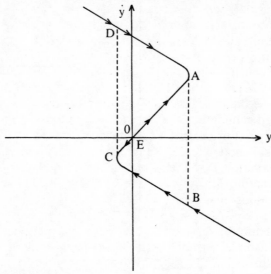

Figure 2.5: The phase solution to Goodwin's nonlinear multiplier–accelerater trade cycle model

cycles with expansions and contractions of different length. He also considers the effects on these cycles of introducing technical progress. In the case outlined above, the introduction of technical progress escapes the peculiarity that it spends more time in depression than boom and the upswing is lengthened and the downswing shortened. The resulting cycle, in the model augmented by technical progress, is a growth cycle, i.e. a cycle around a moving equilibrium.

The interesting possibility provided by nonlinear business cycle modelling is the limit cycle. Such a cycle may repeat itself but need not be regular, in the sense of having identical sequences of deviations above and below the trend, like a sine wave. Thus a limit cycle may have expansions and contractions of different lengths. The limit cycle is around an unstable, and possibly moving, equilibrium; hence the limit cycle is more correctly regarded as the natural state of the economy, as opposed to the moving unstable equilibrium. Thus the limit cycle, rather than the trend growth rate, should be regarded as the natural dynamic motion of the economy. Nonlinear modelling, therefore, allows the cycle to be considered as a natural, endogenous outcome of the economic system, instead of being the response to exogenous shocks which prevent the economy from tracking its stable equilibrium growth path. The role of shocks in limit cycle models is to impart the observed irregularity. This is because if the limit cycle is stable, as Kosobud and O'Neill (1972) have shown analytically and Klein and Preston (1969) have demonstrated numerically, the dynamic path of the shocked economy will eventually return to the path traced by the stable limit cycle.

Nonlinear models can also be used to generate all of the types of solution that linear models can, but linear models cannot generate limit cycles. An example of an interesting nonlinear model that generates a conservative cycle is given in Goodwin (1967). Goodwin's model employs a pair of well-known equations from biology, the Volterra–Lotka equations, to analyse a model of symbiosis of capital and labour. Samuelson (1965, 1967, 1971) discusses the manner in which the Volterra–Lotka model could be converted so that it gives a limit cycle solution. The approach employed by Goodwin is similar to most business cycle modelling, in that the economic theory seems to be designed to force the model solution equation into a form for which well-known results exist, e.g. Rayleigh or van der Pol equations.

Ichmura (1954) provides a useful synthesis of various nonlinear models and the equations that represent their solutions. Gandolfo (1980) also has a useful section on the analysis of nonlinear difference and differential equation cycle models.

Apart from Goodwin's (1951) nonlinear multiplier—accelerator model, perhaps the most influential nonlinear cycle model is that of Kaldor (1940). Kaldor observed that the intersection of the savings and investment functions may yield one of two types of equilibria, stable or unstable, depending on the relative slopes of the savings and investment functions (see Figure 2.6). Kaldor next postulated that the savings and investment functions have sigmoid and inverse sigmoid shapes (see Figure 2.7). He suggested the following reasons for nonlinearity. Considering first the investment function for which, he suggests, dI/dx will be small relative to its 'normal' level for both high and low x. For low x it will be small because there is a great deal of excess capacity, so that an increase in x

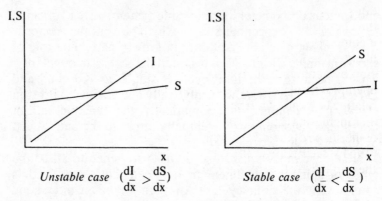

Figure 2.6: Stable and unstable equilibria in investment–savings space

will not necessarily lead to an increase in investment. Investment will not be zero, however, because some (autonomous) investment always occurs. For high x, investment will be small due to rising costs of construction, increasing costs of borrowing, and shortages of funds. The proposed I (x) function is shown in Figure 2.7. Next he considered the savings function, and argued that dS/dx will be large (relative to 'normal') for high and low x. When x is low, savings are cut, and may become negative in order to maintain consumption levels as far as possible. When x is high, agents are likely to save a larger proportion of their income. It can be noted that these considera-

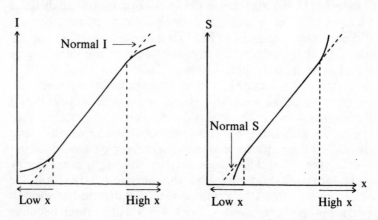

Figure 2.7: Kaldor's investment and savings functions

tions are based on the idea of a 'normal' standard of living, and thus constitute an anticipation of the Duesenberry's 'relative income hypothesis'. Kaldor argued that these tendencies are likely to be reinforced by the fact that low x will imply low employment and a larger proportion of workers living off unemployment benefit, whilst at high x prices will tend to rise relative to wages, and income is distributed in favour of profits, thus increasing the aggregate propensity to savē. The relationship of the shape of the investment function to that used in Goodwin (1951) (see Figure 2.4b) should be noted, as should the fact that the implied, by the savings function, consumption function is an

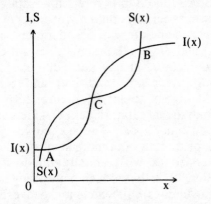

Figure 2.8: Multiple equilibria in investment–savings space

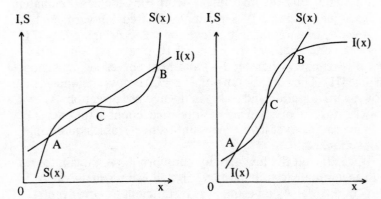

Figure 2.9a: Multiple equilibria with a linear investment function

Figure 2.9b: Multiple equilibria with a linear savings function

anticipation of that implied by the relative income hypothesis (see Duesenberry, 1949). If the savings and the investment functions intersect in the positive quadrant (see Figure 2.8), then there will be three equilibria, two stable (A and B) and one unstable (C). Note also that all that is required is that one of the curves be nonlinear in the described manner since the other could be linear (see Figures 2.9 a and b, which are qualitatively similar to the case depicted in Figure 2.8).

The cycle resulting from Kaldor's model is depicted in Figure 2.10 and may be described as follows. Kaldor argues that the equilibria A and B in Figure 2.8 are stable only in the short run because, as activity continues at either of these points, forces gradually accumulate which render them unstable. This is because $I(x)$ and $S(x)$ both assume constant capital stock, and hence real income, at any particular x. These factors, however, change over time and $I(x)$ and $S(x)$ will shift accordingly. At high x (point B, Figure 2.8), the level of investment is high so that capital stock (k) is increasing and so is the output of consumer goods. The $S(x)$ curve will, therefore, shift upwards, for there is both more saving and consumption for any given x. Also $I(x)$ will gradually shift downwards, since the accumulation of k, by reducing the range of available investment opportunities, will tend to make investment fall. He notes that new innovations will tend to make investment rise, but assumes that the investment depressing factors dominate. Consequently, point B is gradually shifted leftward, and C rightward, thus reducing the level of x and bringing B and C closer to one another (see Figure 2.10, Stage II). The critical point is reached when the $I(x)$ and $S(x)$ curves are tangential (Stage III). The equilibrium point (B+C) is now unstable in the downward direction and stable in the upward direction. After a shock, the level of x will fall rapidly, on account of the excess of ex ante saving over investment, until a new stable equilibrium, A, is reached.

If we start at the low activity equilibrium (A), again forces will accumulate to shift the curves but, this time, in the opposite direction. If, at A, investment is insufficient to cover replacement, yielding negative net induced investment, then investment opportunities accumulate and the $I(x)$ curve will shift upward.

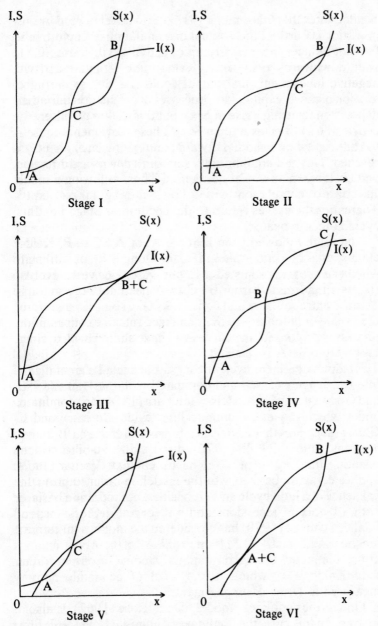

Figure 2.10: The stages of Kaldor's cycle

Kaldor notes that this tendancy is likely to be reinforced by new inventions. Further, the gradual decumulation of capital, in so far as it reduces income per unit of activity, will cause $S(x)$ to shift downwards over time. Kaldor notes that, even with negative investment, real output could rise due to the introduction of more 'capitalistic' processes of production during the depression, causing a rise in $S(x)$; but this makes no difference provided $I(x)$ rises faster than $S(x)$. These movements cause A to shift rightwards and C leftwards until a tangency $(A+C)$ is reached. This new equilibrium is stable in a downward direction, and unstable in an upward direction. Thus, following a shock, an upward cumulation will follow, coming to rest at B. Thereafter the curves return to the position of Stage I and the cycle is then repeated.

The route followed from $B+C$ to A, or $A+C$ to B, Kaldor claims, might be either along $I(x)$, or along $S(x)$, according to whether *ex post* I is adjusted to *ex post* X, or vice versa. He also suggests that the fall from $B+C$ to A need not be very rapid because entreprenaurs and consumers take some time to adjust their scale of purchases to their changed rate of earnings. If the process is prolonged, the curves will have shifted back to Stage IV by the time A is reached.

Kaldor's nonlinear cycle theory has attracted a great deal of interest. It is discussed and compared with the Hicks (1950) and Goodwin (1951) models in Ichmura (1954); the conditions under which it yields a unique limit cycle are discussed by Chang and Smyth (1970); Klein and Preston (1969) and Kosobud and O'Neill (1972) discuss the stability of the resulting limit cycle in a stochastic context; Varian (1979) applies catastrophe theory to the model, in order to prove the existence of a limit cycle and to consider the model as a basis for both a theory of recessions and a theory of depressions; and finally, Schinasi (1979) has considered the model's investment function within an IS—LM framework. All of these contributions utilise the model to explain national income or output, rather than Kaldor's x, which is the level of economic activity measured in terms of employment.

One further nonlinear model, due to Rose (1967), is also of interest. In this case, the nonlinearity imposed is on the Phillips

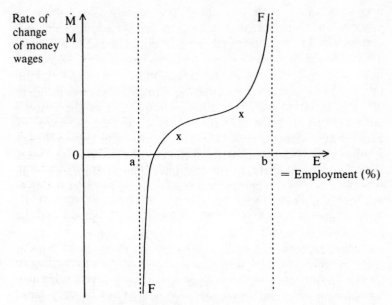

Figure 2.11: Rose's nonlinear Phillips curve

curve, which is depicted in Figure 2.11. Rose demonstrates that his model has a limit cycle solution. The story of the cycle runs as follows. At the minimum level of E, expected demand prices are rising faster than wages (or falling more slowly) and consequently expected profits induce investment and increase employment. The economy moves up the F—F curve (Figure 2.11) towards the flatter region x—x, and once this region is reached there are two alternatives: (i) if expected demand price increases still exceed wage inflation, then investment proceeds, employment continues to rise, and the economy moves up the Phillips curve until wage inflation overtakes the expected demand price increases causing a reversal and a movement back to the flat region x—x; (ii) if, in the region x—x, wage inflation overtakes expected demand price increases, then the economy moves back down the Phillips curve as investment and employment fall. The economy tracks down the curve until wages have fallen sufficiently, relative to expected demand price, to re-stimulate investment.

We can note that, because the economy can go in either of

two directions, once it reaches the region x—x, there is potential in the model for explaining cycles of varying amplitude and period. The variation in this model could be due to variation in the rates of change of expectations, and the analysis would be further complicated by the introduction of price expectations into the Phillips curve necessitating firms to form anticipations of wage inflation based on their anticipations of the unions' anticipations of price inflations. It is clear that the cycle in employment depends critically on the shape of the nonlinear Phillips curve being such that it is not possible to approximate it linearly or log linearly, i.e. it must have a point of inflexion, as was the case for the continuous nonlinear investment function of Goodwin's (1951) model.

In a later article Rose (1969) introduced a money market into his earlier model and considers the relative roles of real and monetary factors in determining the cycle. Desai (1975) finds some evidence in his alternative analysis of the Phillips curve for the shape postulated by Rose, in the period 1914–47, but not in the previous and subsequent periods analysed. Additionally, Desai (1973) and Desai and Shah (1981) investigate further the dynamic properties of Goodwin's (1967) predator—prey model under alternative assumptions.

2.6 THE LIMITATIONS IMPOSED BY THE LINEARITY ASSUMPTION ON CYCLE MODELLING

Goodwin (1955), Kaldor (1954), Marx (1867) and Schumpeter (1935) are prominent amongst a number of economists who have viewed the business cycle and economic growth as inextricably linked, requiring joint explanation, in a theory of economic development.

Linear business cycle modelling usually postulates a (log) linear time trend to represent growth. The statistical analysis of cyles often employs detrended data,[8] where the trend is most commonly calculated using a (log) linear trend or a moving average. Thus, linear modelling leads naturally to the separation of growth and cycle modelling. It is also true, however, that most of the nonlinear cycle models, discussed in Section 2.5, also attempt to explain deviations from assumed (log) linear trends.

There are a number of statistical problems involved in using detrended data to explain cycles. First, due to the Slutsky— Yule[9] effect, taking a moving average may introduce additional oscillations, usually of a longer period than the moving average taken. Perhaps more important for business cycle analysis is the possibility that the (log) linear trend assumption will lead to a biased business cycle (detrended) time series, if there is a shift in the trend. Such shifts could result: from a movement into a different phase of a longer cycle;[10] from a major structural change in the world economy, e.g. following the 1973 and 1979 oil shocks; or from a major policy change. We shall discuss the importance of the latter further when we consider the Lucas (1976) critique of econometric analysis in the next chapter. Haavalmo (1940), in an interesting article on business cycle methodology, warns against being too hasty to insert a linear trend. This is because the trend can appear to improve the fit in a subset of the data[11] and yet when it is incorporated in an extrapolitive predicator it can lead to worse predictions than a model excluding the illusory trend.

The statistical problems arising out of the linearity assumption are not confined to the data, they also relate to the techniques employed in the statistical analysis. Blatt (1978) demonstrates that the analysis of data, generated by a nonlinear Hicks-type model with reasonable[12] parameters imposed using standard linear econometric techniques, yields the conclusion that it was generated by a model that would have a stable solution path if it were not hit by a series of random shocks.

Because nonlinear models yield the possibility of limit cycle solutions and, therefore, of endogenously generated cycles, they should seriously be considered in the next generation of business cycle models. Their potential is also indicated: by the fact that they can also generate all of the solution paths that linear models can; and that it should be possible to devise nonlinear models to explain both the trend (growth) and the cycle, thus avoiding the risks of using detrended data for cycle analysis. Further, the profession has become increasingly familiar with the nonlinear tools required for the theoretical and econometric analyses required. What remains to be undertaken is a serious attempt to locate any of the important nonlinearities that may exist in the economy, and to utilise these functions in a number of statistically testable business cycle models and hypotheses.

2.7 THE ROLE OF THE GOVERNMENT IN THE CYCLE

It was noted in Chapter 1 that Keynesian theorists tended to regard the government as an agency acting on behalf of the public's welfare, by trying to reduce the amplitude of the cycle using counter-cyclical monetary and fiscal policy. The government was not regarded as possessing its own objective function, or at least it was not regarded as having one that conflicted with the public interest.

There were dissenters from this view. Kalecki (1943), in a seminal contribution to the political theory of the business cycle, argued that the government might run the economy in the interest of the dominant, capitalist class.[13] Feiwel (1974) reviews Kalecki's work, and Boddy and Crotty (1975), for example, advocate the stronger proposition that the government's goal is to maximise the long-run profits of the capitalists. Akerman (1947), in some work which may be more closely linked to the modern political theory of the business cycle, discussed in the next chapter, argued that there was a strong relationship between economic and political events. He concluded, from his statistical analysis, that the causal link was from the electoral period – and the political events it brought about – to the economic events. Thus the implication of these various studies was that the government might actually generate the cycle in unemployment, and some other economic variables. This contrasted with the more traditional Keynesian view, expressed for example by Mathews (1969), that, in the UK at least, the government had often accentuated, rather than alleviated, cycles. This was achieved by implementing anti-cyclical policies in such a way that they had their effects in the wrong phase of the cycle. According to this view, this mistiming was neither the result of partisan economic management, nor was it due to negligence on the part of the policy-makers, but rather it was the result of the difficulties of economic management, or 'fine-tuning'. The general Keynesian view, as expressed in Bronfenbrenner (ed.) (1969) and Zarnowitz (ed.) (1972) was that, despite this unintentional mismanagement, Keynesian anti-cyclical demand management policy could, and indeed had, reduced the amplitude of the cycle in the post-war period. Further, it had allowed a period of sustained growth which resulted in a change in the very nature of the cycle to a growth cycle.

Shortly after this consensus had been reached amongst cycle theorists, it was shattered by economic outcomes, and challenged by an alternative, monetarist theory of the cycle. The economic outcomes concerned were the rises in both inflation and unemployment in the late 1960s and early 1970s. These outcomes were seemingly inconsistent with the Phillips (1958) curve, or rather the inflation—unemployment trade-off curve derived from it. They were also inconsistent with the Keynesian demand—pull theory of inflation, derived from the Keynesian cross (income—expenditure) diagram, which concentrates on the goods market. The alternative monetarist theory of the cycle arose out of the work by Friedman and Schwartz (1963a and b), who had been working with monetary data at the NBER.[14] The next section will consider the monetarist theory of the cycle, and its implications for the roles of the government and demand management policy, in the alleviation of the cycle.

2.8 THE MONETARIST I VIEW OF THE BUSINESS CYCLE

The label Monetarist I is coined, from the work of Tobin (1980), to differentiate this view from the Monetarist II, new classical or equilibrium theory of the cycle. The latter is associated with the names of Lucas, Sargent and Barro, and will be discussed in the next chapter.

Friedman and Schwartz (1963a and b) analysed the relationship between the levels of and changes in the money supply and the levels of and changes in nominal national income. They found a strong relationship between changes in the money supply and changes in national income, with the changes in the latter following those in the former after a long and variable lag. The lag was to be taken to be indicative of causality (see

Friedman, 1961; but see also Tobin, 1970). No formal causality testing of the sort discussed in Granger (1969) and Sims (1977, 1980) was undertaken.

If the demonstration of a relationship between money supply growth and national income growth had been all there was to the contribution, then there would have been little fuss. This is because the changes in nominal income could be regarded as changes in aggregate demand, and if, as is common in IS—LM analysis, changes in the money supply were to be regarded as contributing to changes in aggregate demand, then all that had been demonstrated empirically was that changes in the money supply do indeed change aggregate demand, after a long and variable time lag. Friedman and Schwartz, however, went further by trying to establish that inflation is everywhere, and at all times, a monetary phenomenon. Thus the argument was that the change in nominal income, brought about by the change in the money supply, was due solely, after a long and variable lag, to a change in the price level or inflation. The real component of national income would remain unaffected, in the long run, by changes in the money supply. Thus, in the long run, monetary policy would have no real effects, only nominal effects, but, in the short run, the changes in the money supply could have real effects.

The argument is most completely expressed in Friedman (1968) and (1971). In these papers Friedman outlines his monetary theory of nominal income determination and explains the need for a 'missing equation', to split the changes in nominal income into changes in the price level and changes in real income or output. Friedman also discusses the implications of his theory for monetary policy. The 'missing equation' he used was an adaptive expectations (of inflation) augmented Phillips curve (see Figure 2.12). This equation acts like an aggregate supply curve, in that it allows the real and nominal effects of the changes in nominal income that result from changes in the money supply to be determined within the model. In Friedman's analysis no long-run trade-off between wage inflation ($\dot{W}/W$) and unemployment (U) is allowed so that L—L prevails. Any attempt to hold unemployment below its natural rate, (UN), [15] would lead to accelerating inflation. The existence of a short-run trade-off (S_i—S_i) could, however, be

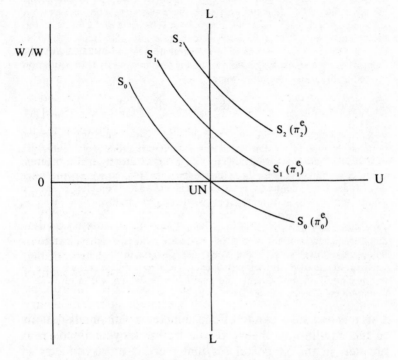

Figure 2.12: The adaptive expectations augmented Phillips curve

Notes:
π_i^e denotes expected inflation and $\pi_2^e > \pi_1^e > \pi_0^e = 0$

exploited by policy-makers. An increase in the money supply could, therefore, increase output and reduce unemployment in the short run, but, after a process of adaptation, inflationary expectations would adjust and these real effects would disappear at the cost of higher inflation. The only way that unemployment could be held below its natural rate, in this model, is by repeating the monetary stimulus regularly and, thereby, continually fuelling higher inflation. The mechanism by which the changes in the money supply have real effects on unemployment is described by Friedman (1968, p. 10) as follows:

'An increase in the growth of the money supply will leave people with higher nominal balances than they desire and, in a portfolio adjustment, there will be a fall in interest rates. In this and other ways spending will be stimulated and income will rise. This will initially take the form of a rise in output and employment, rather than prices. People have been expecting prices to be stable and prices and wages have been set for some time in the future on this basis. It takes time for people to adjust to the new state of demand. Producers will tend to react to the expansion in aggregate demand by raising output, employees by working longer hours, and the unemployed by taking jobs now offered at the former nominal wage.

These are, however, only the initial effects, he argues,

because selling prices of products typically respond to an unanticipated rise in nominal demand faster than the prices of factors of production, real wages received have gone down – though real wages anticipated by employees went up, since employees implicitly evaluated the wages offered at the earlier price level. Indeed, the simultaneous fall *ex post* in real wages to employers and rise *ex ante* in real wages to employees is what enabled employment to increase. But the decline in *ex post* real wages will soon come to affect anticipations. Employees will start to reckon on rising prices of the things they buy and to demand higher nominal wages for the future. 'Market' unemployment is below the 'natural' level. There is an excess demand for labour, so real wges will tend to rise towards their initial level. The rise in real wages will reverse the decline in unemployment, and lead to a rise, which will in turn return unemployment to its former level.

This mechanism is of interest, in connection with our discussion of the equilibrium theory of the business cycle in the next chapter, in that it postulates that there is an asymmetry of information at the basis of the adjustment process.

With respect to the cycles in unemployment, output and inflation, a full explanation clearly requires a detailed analysis of the causes of the long and variable lags in the effects of monetary policy. This implies that an analysis of the transmission mechanism, through which monetary policy effects real and nominal variables, is needed. Such an analysis is not attempted in detail anywhere in Friedman's published work, and is usually dismissed, after a brief discussion, as a problem requiring further consideration. As a first approximation, Friedman usually assumes that changes in the money supply result from random distributions of notes (rather than coins, we hope), from a helicopter. This sidesteps a number of important issues pertaining to the channels through which the money supply actually enters the economy, and the possibility that money entering through one channel might have a different effect from that entering through another, due to distribution effects.

Friedman's discussions of the transmission mechanism are, however, similar in many respects to Keynesian ones, in that a change in the supply of money alters the portfolio of assets held by agents receiving the money. Portfolio adjustment is required (see Friedman, 1961), and, if money is used to purchase short-term interest bearing assets, for example, then their prices and interest rates will change. This will alter the relative attractiveness of short-term financial assets, when compared with longer-term financial assets, and so on. Thus there will be a whole series of interest rate changes, spreading from shorter to longer-term financial assets, and culminating when portfolio adjustment is complete. The adjustment is thus achieved through interest rate changes and these changes may have an effect on the economy in the traditional Keynesian manner, e.g. through influences on investment. The major difference between Friedman and Keynesians lies in the range of assets composing the portfolio. Friedman argues that portfolios normally include not only financial assets but also non-financial assets, such as consumer durables. In the latter case the interest rate will be related to the price of services provided by these assets. Hence, a change in the money supply might have a direct effect on consumption in the course of the portfolio adjustment.

The main implication of Friedman's contribution, for monetary policy, is that the money supply should be constrained to grow at a fixed rate, in line with output or productivity growth perhaps.[16] This was because its effects on the economy were large and somewhat unpredictable and consequently it was better to keep the money supply well under control, rather than use it in a discretionary manner for active stabilisation policy.

The effect of the debate between Friedman and the Keynesians was to produce a neoclassical synthesis (see Patinkin, 1965), in which the natural rate hypothesis seemed to be accepted and arguments about the income and interest rate elasticities of the IS and LM curves, and their underlying functions, were matters to be resolved empirically.

The role of fiscal policy in cycle stabilisation also required critical examination in the light of Friedman's contributions and those of other economists. The acknowledgement of the need to take account of the budget constraint,[17] in economic modelling, forced economists to consider how the effects of fiscal policy differed according to the method by which the budget deficit was financed. For example, a fiscal expansion can be tantamount to a monetary expansion, if the increased budget deficit is financed by borrowing from commercial banks. A fiscal expansion might, however, have different effects if it was financed by borrowing from abroad or by borrowing in the bonds market. Borrowing in the bonds market would probably push up the rate of interest which might in turn discourage investment, and perhaps consumption, so that the stimulating effect of the fiscal expansion might be reduced. This observation sparked off the 'crowding-out' debate, which was essentially about the size of the fiscal multiplier under bond financing. The IS—LM model acknowledges some crowding-out in that the multiplier effects of an expansion in the budget deficit are less when the money and goods market are considered jointly than when the goods market is considered in isolation. The multiplier effect of the expansionary fiscal policy is still deemed to be greater than one, however. A number of economists, however, argued that the crowding-out effect was larger than that assumed in Keynesian models, so that the multiplier might be less than one – almost zero, or even negative in some of the more extreme arguments.[18] As was the case with many of the issues raised in the debates between Keynesian and Monetarists I, these issues were more likely to be settled empirically than theoretically.

2.9 SUMMARY AND CONCLUSION

In this chapter a number of competing theories of the business cycle postulated in the 1936 to 1975 period have been reviewed. The theories can be roughly classified according to whether the modelling procedure adopted was linear or non-linear and stochastic or deterministic. In the real world, stochastic formulations would appear to be the more realistic, but the introduction of stochastic terms restricts the usefulness of linear formulations and increases the attractiveness of nonlinear formulations. This is because the conservative solution to the linear model becomes unviable, because of its explosiveness, and because nonlinear models introduce the possibility of stable, even under random shocks, limit cycle solutions. This is only true, however, if one is looking for an endogenous theory of the cycle. If the Frischian view is accepted, then the linear formulation is adequate. Since the possibility of an endogenous theory of the cycle seems to rest on the existence of a stable limit cycle, the onus is on the proponents of such a cycle to use nonlinear econometric techniques to identify the major non-linearities in the economy. The theories reviewed in this chapter provide some suggestions concerning the location of these nonlinearities, but they could be in other sectors of the economy. There is no guarantee that economic relationships can all be adequately approximated by linear relationships.

Most of the models reviewed have been Keynesian in origin and have relied on consumption—investment behaviour, or wage—price profit interactions, to explain the business cycle. Little account was taken by them of the effects of the growth in the money supply on the cycle. It was left to Friedman and his followers to try to redress the balance by advocating the case that changes in the money supply played a prime role in bringing about the changes in real and nominal economic variables that we call the business cycle. This contribution was discussed in the previous section of this chapter. The net result was the view, embodied in the 'neoclassical synthesis', that the early Keynesian modelling had been remiss in ignoring the monetary sector in its business cycle modelling.

The next chapter consists of a review of the major contributions to the business cycle literature in the post-1975 period. Wherever possible these contributions will be related to those discussed in this chapter.

3 Business Cycle Modelling Post-1975

3.1 INTRODUCTION

In 1975 there were two major contributions to the business cycle literature: Lucas (1975) presented an 'equilibrium business cycle' (EBC) theory; and Nordhaus (1975) presented a 'political business cycle' (PBC) theory. Neither theory was without roots in the literature: Lucas (1977) cites Hayek (1933), and Nordhaus (1975) cites Kalecki (1943), as having discussed the issues previously. But both contributions were exemplary in applying new methods to old problems and, consequently, had a major impact and captured the imagination of business cycle students. The two theories are contradictory and complementary in a number of aspects, and these features will be highlighted as each theory is discussed in turn. In particular, they are contradictory with respect to the assumptions that are made about the electorate and the role of the government in the business cycle. The PBC theory assumes that voters form their expectations about potential economic outcomes myopically, whilst the EBC theory endows economic agents with rationally formed expectations on the basis of knowledge of the true economic model. The PBC theory gives the government a major causal role in generating the cycle, whilst in the EBC theory the government only influences the cycle by generating random monetary shocks. The theories are, however, complementary in their implications for the development of business cycle theory: they both seem to indicate that the government needs to be endogenised in cycle models and that a game

38

theoretic treatment of the interaction between the government and other economic agents is required.

In Sections 3.2 and 3.3, respectively, the EBC and PBC theories will be discussed; and in Section 3.4 a summary and some conclusions will be presented.

3.2 THE EQUILIBRIUM THEORY OF THE BUSINESS CYCLE

The new classical economics, or Monetarism II in Tobin's (1980) terminology, replaced the adaptive expectations hypothesis (AEH), used by Friedman and other adherents to Monetarism I and Keynesians alike, by the Muth (1961) rational expectations hypothesis (REH). When combined with the natural rate hypothesis (NRH) and the assumptions of perfect competition and continuous market clearing, the REH led to powerful implications for monetary policy, akin to those derived by pre-Keynesian, classical economists. By utilising the joint RE—NR hypotheses, as well as the continuous market clearing assumption, it was demonstrated that money had a neutral effect on real economic variables. The demonstrations used simple economic models incorporating an aggregate supply function, a money supply generating/feedback rule, and IS and LM curves, to represent aggregate demand. The most famous contributions were those of Sargent and Wallace (1975, 1976). In addition to demonstrating that anticipated changes in the money supply would have no real effects, even in the short run and that they could only lead to changes in the price level or inflation, they advocated that the money supply should be as predicatable as possible. Thus they concurred with Friedman's view, that money should follow a fixed growth rate rule. The reason for their advocacy of this rule was not the same as Friedman's. Friedman (1974) had argued that because money had a powerful influence on the economy and because the effects of a change in the rate of growth of the money supply were only realised after a long and variable lag, it was better to keep the money supply growing at a fixed rate. In contrast, Sargent and Wallace argued that unanticipated changes in the price level affect real variables, and output in particular, and that a major cause of these shock changes in prices were the unanticipated changes to the money supply. Thus, if the money supply could be made as predicatable as possible, then a major source of economic instability could be removed. In their view, monetary policy should not, and indeed could not, be used for short-run economic stabilisation, since under the REH Friedman's short-run trade-off between inflation and unemployment (i.e. the Phillips curve) no longer existed. This is partly because, under the REH, Friedman's assumed asymmetry of information between firms and workers, discussed in the previous chapter, disappears; at least if one assumes that the costs of collecting and processing information are zero, so that the workers, or their hired representatives, the unions, and the firms would share the same information sets and form their expectations accordingly.

Underlying the work of Sargent and Wallace is the Lucas (1973) supply hypothesis, which may be written as follows:

$$y_t = y_{nt} + a(p_t - p_t^*) + e_t; \ a > 0 \qquad 3.1$$

where y_t is the $\log_e$ of output at time t and y_{nt} is its natural rate; p_t is the $\log_e$ of the price level and p_t^* is its rational expectation conditional on information available up to period $t-1$, i.e. $E_t(P_t \mid \Omega_{t-1})$ where Ω_{t-1} is the information set at time $t-1$; e_t is a random error process, and a is a constant parameter. y_{nt} is often, as a first approximation, taken to be represented by a log linear trend, i.e.:

$$y_{nt} = \delta + \gamma t \qquad 3.2$$

Thus a natural (log) linear growth is assumed and the business cycle theory aims to explain the deviations of output from this growing natural rate. Cyclical output (y_{ct}) is then defined as:

$$y_{ct} = y_t - y_{nt} \qquad 3.3$$

Using Equation 3.1 it is clear that:

$$y_{ct} = a(p_t - p_t^*) + e_t; \ a > 0 \qquad 3.4$$

and since e_t and $(p_t - p_t^*)$ are both random processes, under rational expectations, y_{ct} should itself be a random process.

Because the existence of the business cycle implies that there should be serial correlation in the y_{ct} series, equation 3.4

is unlikely to form a basis for an explanation of the business cycle. Lucas (1977) and Sargent (1979) accept that, in addition to the need to explain the serial correlation in the observed y_{ct} series, a new classical, or equilibrium, theory of the business cycle must also be able to explain a number of 'stylised' facts about the movements and co-movements of various other economic times series, as documented by the NBER. It is to these problems that Lucas addressed himself formally, in his 1975 paper, and more discursively, in his 1977 paper.

Equation 3.1 may be reformulated, to include a lagged output term, as follows:

$$y_t = y_{nt} + \alpha(p_t - p_t^*) + \beta_{t-1} + \varepsilon_t \qquad 3.5$$

then, using the lag operator L, such that $Ly_t = y_{t-1}$, the following equation can be derived:

$$y_t = (1-\beta L)^{-1} y_{nt} + \alpha(1-\beta L)^{-1} (p_t - p_t^*) + (1 - \beta L)^{-1} \varepsilon_t$$

$$3.6$$

Letting $y_{nt}' = (1-\beta L)^{-1} y_{nt}$, and assuming $o < \beta < 1$, gives:

$$y_t = y_{nt}' + \alpha \sum_{i=0}^{\infty} \beta^i (p_{t-i} - p_{t-i}^*) + \sum_{i=0}^{\infty} \beta^i \varepsilon_t \qquad 3.7$$

Alternatively, introducing y_{ct-1} into equation 3.4 gives:

$$y_{ct} = \alpha \sum_{i=0}^{\infty} \beta^i (p_{t-i} - p_{t-i}^*) + \sum_{i=0}^{\infty} \beta^i \varepsilon_t \qquad 3.8$$

The supply equation is now transformed so that a weighted average, with geometrically declining weights, of all past shocks now affect current cyclical output. The effects of shocks persist over time and are capable of explaining the serial correlation in output. The first task facing the EBC theorists was then to justify the inclusion of y_{ct-1} (or y_{t-1}) in the supply hypothesis, by explaining the channels of persistence. Note that, as Lucas and Sargent (1978) later acknowledged, the Frischain modelling framework, discussed in Chapter 1, is being adopted since they are seeking a propagation model to transform the (random in this case) shocks into a cycle. Further, they have chosen a (log) linear framework which allows an easy docomposition of (natural) growth theory and cycle theory. In common with most business cycle models, the explanation of the (natural) growth rate is left for future discussion. Thus no full theory of the determination of the natural rates, of output and unemployment in particular, or their movements over time is offered.

The explanation, chosen by Lucas (1975), of the persistence in the effects of monetary and other shocks, was based on an imperfect information story. Economic agents are viewed as operating in 'island' markets (indexed z) which are subject to local, real shocks and aggregate, nominal monetary shocks. The statistical distributions of these shocks are assumed to be known but the actual realisations of the current shocks are assumed to be unobservable. The agents can move between the 'island' markets randomly, at the end of each period, but capital stocks remain in place. The information set possessed by all agents in each particular 'island' market includes knowledge of the current, market clearing, price in the 'island' market but excludes knowledge of the market clearing price in each of the other 'island' markets. Additionally, it was assumed by Lucas (1975) that there are no globally traded assets and, therefore, there are no observable market clearing prices for such assets.

Under these conditions price changes convey signals about changing market conditions. A local producer facing a price increase will know that a supply reaction might be required. The producer's reaction will depend on whether the price increase is interpreted as a favourable change in the relative price of the product or whether it is the result of a general, inflationary increase in all prices. In the former case a supply response is required and in the latter it is not, but the nature of any supply response will also depend on whether the price change is believed, by the producer, to be permanent or temporary. Lucas, therefore, sets up an information structure in which the producer faces a 'signal extraction problem', a term borrowed from engineering, in that the price change gives a signal from which information has to be extracted before a response can be made.

Lucas postulates a strong positive supply response, by producers, to a small change in relative prices, even if it is judged to be temporary, because of the opportunities for profit offered. Lucas (1977) discusses these issues, in connection with the EBC theory, in some detail and argues that there will also be a positive supply response by labour to a small increase in wages. The theoretical underpinnings of the 'islands' market story and the postulated positive supply responses to price and wage increases lie in the 'new microeconomics', discussed in Phelps (ed.) (1972) and in the work of Lucas and Rapping (1969).

In order to attempt to resolve the signal extraction problem the rational, in the sense of Muth (1961), agents use past information and knowledge of the distributions of the real and nominal shocks. From this they form an expectation of the current market clearing price, in market island z, i.e. $p_t^e(z)$, and, if the actual market clearing price, in market island z, i.e. $p_t(z)$, exceeds $p_t^e(z)$, then output will be increased. Lucas (1975) demonstrates that the larger the variance in the money supply, the less likely are agents to interpret observed price changes as changes in relative prices, and the smaller will be the supply response.

The role of competition in the model is to force agents to react quickly to price increases in their pursuit of profit maximisation. If agents wait to see whether a price increase really is a relative, rather than an absolute, one, then they will have missed a profitable opportunity because other agents will have responded more quickly. The perfect competition assumption also gives the implication that market clearing prices can be assumed to be known.

Lucas's (1975) model is, therefore, capable of explaining positive supply responses to unanticipated price increases, but a business cycle model needs, additionally, to explain the persistence in the effects of the price shocks on output. In order to explain why serial correlation in output might result, a version of the accelerator is invoked by Lucas (1975). The unanticipated price increase raises the sales expectations of the producer, who will increase output, in so far as there is spare capacity, and may even reduce inventories. If these responses are impossible, or undesirable, then investment will be undertaken in order to increase productive capacity. If a rigid relationship between investment and expected output growth is postulated, then an accelerator relationship, similar to the

Keynesian one based on a constant capital-output ratio and relating investment to actual output growth, is implied. By incorporating this accelerator into his model, Lucas (1975) is able to demonstrate that business cycles can be generated in a competitive economy, with continuous market clearing, where all agents hold rationally formed expectations and the natural rate hypothesis holds. The Lucas (1975) paper gives the first major formulation of the EBC theory, but it is rather difficult, mathematically, to follow and the Lucas (1977) paper can be recommended, both because it is easier to read and because it discusses a number of the main points in more detail.

To recapitulate, the two key aspects of Lucas's theory are: the modelling of the information structure, which poses the signal extraction problem; and the accelerator, which explains the persistence of the effects of the price shocks. On both counts the theory has been criticised and generalised. Consequently, it is instructive to discuss each of these aspects in more detail.

The hypothesised information structure is clearly very artificial and the exclusion of globally-traded assets, such as bonds, equities or foreign currencies, is not a step towards realism. In Lucas's (1975, p. 1120, footnote 8) words: 'It is intended simply to capture in a tractable way the fact that economic activity offers a succession of ambiguous, unanticipated opportunities which cannot be expected to stay fixed while more information is collected.' Lucas (1975) speculates that the inclusion of a bond market in his model would modify, but probably not eliminate, the cycle. Karni (1980) examines this proposition within Lucas's one (global) shock framework, and finds that if the market price of the globally-traded asset, in this case the rate of interest (R_t), can be observed, by all the 'island' market traders, then the signal extraction problem will be diffused. This is because, with one global (monetary) shock and one local (real) shock and two observed market clearing prices, the local and the global, there are two equations in two unknown shocks. It is to be noted that the effects of the local shocks are, essentially, averaged out in the global market, so that any deviation of R_t from its expected value is due to the global, monetary shock alone. The two equations are derived from the assumed knowledge of the means and the variances of the two shocks, which allow expectations of R_t and $P_t(z)$ to be formed. These two equations can be solved, for the two unknown shocks, allowing the agents to decide what proportion of the local price change is due to the local shock and what proportion is due to the global shock. In order to retain the signal extraction problem it is sufficient to have more global shocks than observations on market clearing prices, of globally-traded assets, which give independent information on the various global shocks. Barro (1981), in his useful survey of EBC theory, observed that some of these global shocks could be real, rather than nominal, e.g. the effects of wealth or sunspots.

Barro (1980) also considers the effects of introducing a global capital market into his (1976) model. The latter is not a complete EBC model, in that the persistence of the effects of the monetary shocks are not explained, but it does demonstrate that only the unanticipated growth in the money supply affects output under the RE and NR hypotheses. The introduction of the globally–traded asset, and the observation of its market clearing price, does not fundamentally alter the conclusions derived from the model, provided that a second aggregate shock is introduced into the model to supplement the aggregate money supply shock. The shock introduced by Barro is via a random error term added to the aggregate money demand equation. Thus Barro (1980) confirms that the introduction of observations on the market clearing prices on globally-traded assets does not diffuse the signal extraction problem faced by agents, provided that extra shocks are introduced.

In these models the problem remains to explain why agents do not go on sampling and observing prices from all other local markets if it is so important to them to solve the signal extraction problem. This would be the rational response if information was costless to collect and process. Lucas (1975, p. 1120, footnote 8) observes that the problem could be 'slightly mitigated by the purchase of additional information'. There must, therefore, be an implicit assumption that costs to collecting and processing information exist, in which case agents would collect and process information up to the point where the marginal cost equalled the marginal benefit from doing so. What needs to be explained is why marginal cost equals marginal benefit when only the local price of the market, in which the agent is operating at the time, is observed. Furthermore, it is doubtful that information on even the market clearing local price is available, let alone costlessly provided by some, market-specific, Walrasian auctioneer. Many economists, especially those belonging to the so-called disequilibrium school[1] would argue that market clearing prices are not observable. Instead, firms tend to set prices and output responses result from quantity signals, such as changes in orders and fluctuations in inventory stocks around their optimum. Additionally, the 'islands' abstraction eliminates interdependence between markets, since they are all assumed to clear individually at all times. Many economists have, however, argued that the interdependence of markets is a crucial factor in the generation of business cycles and in the understanding of the co-movements between the economic time series involved. It is also a cornerstone to the understanding of the workings of the multiplier, since it explains how a reduction in income affects unemployment in the Keynesian analysis.[2]

Lucas's (1975) explanation of persistence and the justification of the inclusion of the lagged independent variable in the supply hypothesis will next be considered. It will be recalled that the accelerator was ued to explain persistence, so that the lagged value of the capital stock might replace y_{t-1}, in equation 3.5, in some formulations. Barro (1981) reviews some of the alternative channels of persistence that have been considered. These include inventory stocks of finished goods, work in progress, raw materials, etc., wage contracts, other contracts (see Okun, 1980), information lags, etc. The general idea is that anything that can explain why agents cannot react to shocks as they occur, and when they want to, or anything that locks them into a reaction to a particular shock over a period when other shocks are occurring, can explain persistence.

Kydland and Prescott (1977, 1980, 1982) have also attempted to explain the serial correlation in output, using equilibrium models. These models differ from EBC models generated by monetary shocks in that they also consider cycles generated by technological changes and fiscal policy changes. Their (1982) model, which is one of the few EBC models to proceed to econometric formulation and estimation, uses fabrication lags[3] to explain the persistence in the effects of the shocks.

In conclusion, the EBC theory respresents an ingenious attempt to explain the business cycle in a world where markets are assumed to clear continuously, agents are endowed with rationally formed expectations, and the natural rate hypothesis holds. Attempts to test the theory, apart from that of Kydland and Prescott (1982) which estimates some of the parameters of an EBC model on the basis of guestimates of others, have been aimed at testing the underlying hypotheses, of the REH and the NRH, sometimes separately, but ususally jointly. The outcomes of these various tests will be reviewed in the next chapter.

Before proceeding to a discussion of the political theory of the business cycle, note should be taken of an additional major contribution by Lucas. Lucas (1976) provides a critique of the policy analysis, usually undertaken by economists, based on the implications of the REH. He argues that policy analysis, based on the values of estimated multipliers or utilising simulation procedures, will be valueless when agents are endowed with rationally formed expectations, especially when the policies under analysis represent major deviations from past policies. This is because the parameters of the model, used to estimate the multipliers and in the simulation analysis, are based on estimates using historical data covering periods in which the policy being analysed was not in use. Given that rational agents are likely to respond to policy changes, the parameters of the model are also likely to change. Hence, the historically estimated parameter estimates cannot be used for policy analysis. This has major implications for the manner in which the government should instigate its policy in the face of business cycle fluctuations. If the government decides to be active, it must not simply take the economic model to have fixed parameters and then try to maximise its objective function, which we shall assume to be the economy's welfare function for the present, subject to the fixed economic constraints in the manner envisaged by Theil (1968), for example. Instead the government must allow for a response by the rational agents, to its policy initiative, which will alter the parameters of the model. Further, the government must also allow for the fact that the rational agents know that the government, in choosing its policy, is taking account of their likely response to it and that they will react accordingly, and so on. What seems to be required is a full game theoretic analysis of government policy setting. The crude assumption, made in pre-REH days, that the government is playing a game against nature, in the form of a fixed economic environment, is no longer tenable. This latter observation, of Lucas's, has spawned a number of policy debates: on the relative merits of rules versus discretion, in policy setting, and of fixed versus flexible policy rules. These, often highly technical, debates will not be considered in this book, however.[4]

3.3 THE POLITICAL THEORY OF THE BUSINESS CYCLE

The political business cycle (PBC) theory emphasises the role of the government, or state, in the generation of business cycles. Nordhaus's (1975) article sparked renewed interest in this area, which had drifted out of mainstream economics and had come to be regarded as a topic pertaining to the subject of political economy. Nordhaus drew attention to the need for reconsideration of the role of the objective function of the government, and its implications for macroeconomic theory and the business cycle. Downs (1957) argued that the government, like other agents, should be viewed as a utility maximiser and that the utility of the government was more closely related to electoral support than general economic welfare, assumed, for example by Theil (1968) in traditional Keynesian policy analyses. The government would, therefore, pursue vote maximisation in its attempt to maximise utility, because its utility depends on being in office. The PBC theory argues that, in order to maximise its vote share, or minimise the reduction in stock of votes held on election (see MacRae, 1977), the government might create a cycle, in output, unemployment and inflation, for example. The conditions under which the government can do this depend primarily on an assumption that the electorate behaves myopically, in the sense that they do not vote strategically.[5] The electorate are assumed to have decaying memories of past economic events, even within the electoral period, and to vote on the most recent economic outcomes. Further, they are assumed to be unable to forecast the effects of current policies on economic conditions in the next electoral period, granting that some of the effects of the policies are realised only after a time lag. The electorate are, therefore, not endowed with rational expectations or with knowledge of the true workings of the economy. The government is thus, in a sense, able to create a cycle by fooling the electorate.

The period and regularity of the induced cycle is dependent on the electoral period. With a fixed presidential electoral period, as in the USA, one might expect to observe a fairly regular cycle if the theory had any substance, although the pattern might be complicated by the need to take account of the congressional elections, in addition to the presidential elections. In both the Nordhaus (1975) and the MacRae (1977) formulations of the PBC theory, the government aims to optimise subject to an economic constraint, which is an inflation—unemployment trade-off curve. The objectives are also couched in terms of manipulating inflation and unemployment to win votes, and the cycle generated is in these two variables. Under the PBC one would expect falling inflation and rising unemployment following an election, and the reverse as the election approached. The fixed electoral period should condition these movements, in inflation and unemployment, into a cycle. Thus, the cycle involved might be called an electoral economic cycle, to differentiate it from contributions to PBC theory related to the seminal contribution of Kalecki (1943). The basis of the Nordhaus and MacRae electoral (or modern) PBC theory lies, more correctly, with the work of Akerman (1944, 1946, 1947). Akerman analysed relationships between economic and political events, considered the view that economic events affected political events, but then concluded that political events caused economic events. He analysed electorally-induced cycles using US, UK, German and French data.

The Kalecki PBC theory is more political in the sense that it views the state's role in the generation of the cycle as the result of its partisan management of the capitalist economic system on behalf of the dominant capitalist class. Kalecki was influenced by both Marx and Keynes, among other economists of course. He argued that Keynesian theory had demonstrated the possibility of the achievement of continuous full employment, but that such a policy would not necessarily be in the interest of, and would be opposed by, capitalists. The state of continuous full employment would, therefore, require a change in the social order. Given the capitalists' oppostion to continuous full employment, and their appreciation of attempts made by the government to alleviate recessions, Kalecki expected to see the state presiding over a cycle in unemployment. The state would alleviate it, in recessions, but prevent the continuation of the full employment achieved in the following booms. Kalecki's work on the PBC theory is usefully reviewed by Feiwel (1974). A related contribution is that of Boddy and Crotty (1975), who argue that the state runs the economy in order to maximise long-run aggregate profits, and does so by creating a cycle in unemployment using fiscal and monetary policy. They support their thesis using US profits data and examining profits in each of the stages of the NBER reference cycle.[6] They found that, in the post-second world war period in which Keynesian policies were dominant, the profits share of income, and the absolute level of profits, had fallen in the latter half of each expansion. Correspondingly wages and the wage share had risen. They view the erosion of profits as 'the result of successful class struggle waged by labour against capital – struggle that is confined and ultimately reversed by the relaxation of demand and the rise in unemployment engineered by the capitalists and acquiesced to and abetted by the state.' They point out that high unemployment is of no use for conditioning workers' behaviour, since it simply creates an unemployed class. Fluctuating unemployment, with occasional full employment is, however, desirable for the conditioning of workers in the interests of capitalism, because it maintains work skills and keeps alive the threat of unemployment to those in work.

The modern electoral theory of the cycle, associated with the work of Nordhaus and MacRae, is discussed next in more detail. Taking Nordhaus's (1975) contribution first, Nordhaus assumed that the government aims to maximise a vote function subject to a set of economic constraints. The vote function postulated is:

$$V_\theta = \int_0^\theta g(u_t, \pi_t) e^{\mu t} dt \qquad 3.9$$

where $g(u_t, \pi_t)$ assumes that votes depend on unemployment (u) and inflation (π), θ is the length of the electoral period, and μ is the rate of decay of voters' memories. The myopic behaviour of voters is explicit in that their votes only depend on the economic outcomes in the electoral period, expected future outcomes have no influence. Further, $\mu > 0$ ensures that the most recent economic outcomes are given a higher weight in influencing voting behaviour at an election. Figure 3.1 depicts the assumed weighting system, the weights increase from the beginning of the electoral period, from F to A, and then at the end of the electoral period drop to zero, i.e. from A to B.

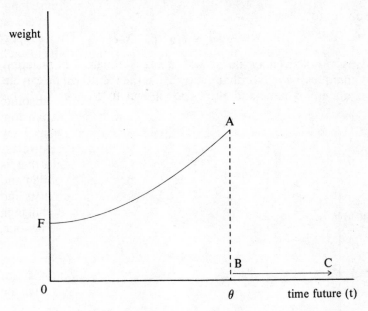

Figure 3.1: Weights attached to economic performance in the Nordhaus model

The postulated economic constraints are:

$$\pi_t = f(u_t) + \lambda v_t \qquad\qquad 3.10$$
$$\dot{v}_t = \gamma(\pi_t - v_t) \qquad\qquad 3.11$$

where v is the expected rate of inflation, so that equation 3.10 is an inflation augmented Phillips curve, in terms of prices rather than wages, and equation 3.11 describes and adaptive expectations formation mechanism. To give the model explicit form, in order to allow solution, it is assumed that:

$$g(u,\pi) = -u^2 - \beta\pi ; \qquad \pi \geq 0, \beta > 0 \qquad 3.12$$

and

$$f(u) = \alpha_0 - \alpha_1 u \qquad\qquad 3.13$$

The problem for the government is then to maximise V_θ, where:

$$V_\theta = \int_0^\theta [-\beta\alpha_0 - u^2 + \beta\alpha_1 u - \beta\lambda v]e^{\mu t}dt \qquad 3.14$$

subject to:

$$\dot{v} = \gamma [\alpha_0 - \alpha_1 u - (1-\lambda)v] \qquad 3.15$$

This problem may be solved using standard optimisation techniques,[7] and Nordhaus shows that the result will be a cycle in unemployment and prices as shown in Figure 3.2. The

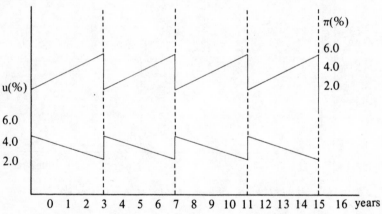

Figure 3.2: Nordhaus's cycle in unemployment and inflation

typical cycle, therefore, runs as follows: immediately after an election the victor will raise unemployment to some relatively high rate in order to combat inflation; then, as elections approach, the unemployment rate will be lowered to the purely myopic point. The key target variable for the government is assumed to be unemployment, and the cycle in inflation is generated as a by-product, due to the assumed inflation—unemployment trade-off.

Some explanation of the purely myopic unemployment rate is in order. Nordhaus takes the social welfare function to be:

$$W = \int_0^\infty g(u_t, \pi_t)e^{-\rho t}dt \qquad 3.16$$

where ρ is the discount rate. If the economic contraints are taken to be those described by equations 3.10 and 3.11, then the long-run optimum solution can be shown diagrammatically. Figure 3.3 shows the contours of the aggregate voting function, $V_t = g(u_t, \pi_t)$. Each contour represents the locus of all combinations of π and u that would net a particular fraction of the total

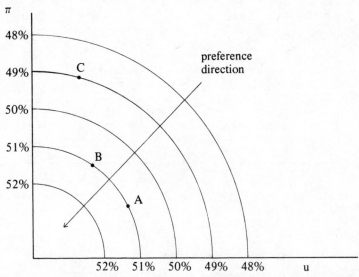

Figure 3.3: Isovote lines in inflation—unemployment space

electoral vote. Lower combinations of π and u net a larger vote share than a higher combination of π and u. Thus the combinations of π and u implied by points A and B are preferred to that implied by C. There is also a trade-off between inflation and unemployment in the electorate's preferences, so that the two different combinations of π and u, implied by points A and B, net the same electoral support. Nordhaus's assumption regarding the adaptive expectations augmented Phillips curve are depicted in Figure 3.4. Note that the long-run Phillips curve (L—L) implies less of a trade-off than the short-run Phillips curves (S_i—S_j), but that it is not vertical. The position of the short-run Phillips curve is dependent on the level of expected inflation v. The higher is v the higher is the short-run Phillips curve.

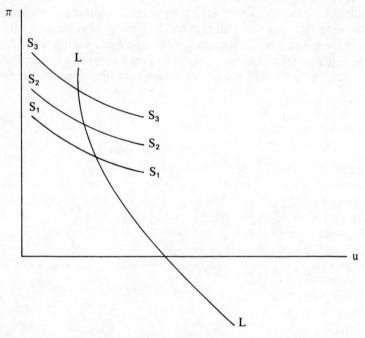

Figure 3.4: Long-and short-run Phillips curves

The isovote-share lines, from Figure 3.3, and the Phillips curves, from Figure 3.4, can be put together, as in Figure 3.5. Solving the problem of maximising welfare, subject to the economic constraints, yields a number of special cases, according to the assumed parameter values. If $\rho = 0$, so that the planners do not use discounting in allocating resources between future and present generations, the golden rule policy solution (u^G, π^G) prevails. This occurs where the long-run Phillips curve is tangent to the aggregate voting function, at point G. At the

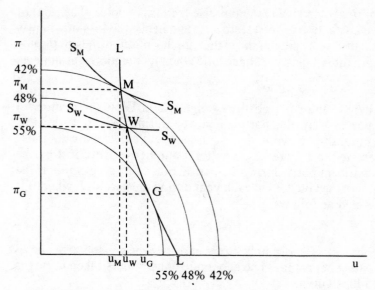

Figure 3.5: Solutions to Nordhaus's model

opposite extreme is the case $\rho = \infty$, i.e. where the planners apply infinite discount rates in evaluating policy. This gives the myopic solution, in which the welfare of future generations is ignored. This occurs at point M, where the short-run Phillips curve (S_M–S_M) is tangent to the aggregate voting function. M lies to the north-west of G, so that myopic policies have higher inflation and lower unemployment than golden rule policies. A third outcome is also of interest: the general welfare optimum solution, at W. This lies between M and G and occurs where the slope of the aggregate voting function is intermediate between the long-run trade-off (L—L) and the short-run trade-off (S_w–S_w)

In addition to analysing the short-run solution, which yields the PBC, Nordhaus also examines long-run choice in democratic systems. He finds that the asymptotic behaviour of the system, over the course of many electoral regimes, is towards a policy on L—L that has lower u and higher π than optimal, i.e. further up L—L than point W. He further shows that the asymptotic policy is in fact the myopic one.

MacRae (1977) analyses a similar problem. In this case the

political objective is to minimise the loss of votes. The level of dissatisfaction of the electorate, and hence the loss of votes, is assumed to be greater the higher are the inflation and unemployment rates, π and u. A quadratic vote loss function is assumed:[8]

$$W(\pi_t,u_t) = \tfrac{1}{2}q\pi_t^2 + \tfrac{1}{2}ru_t^2 \qquad 3.17$$

where q and r are positive weights, and W_t is the number of votes lost by the party in power during year t. From this relationship isovote lines can be derived, similar to those depicted in Figure 3.3. The total number of votes lost by the incumbent party during the period preceding an election is the sum of the vote loss in each year during the period, J, where J is defined as follows:

$$J = \sum_{i=1}^{N} W(\pi_t,u_t) \qquad 3.18$$

where N is the number of years between elections, and is assumed constant. The economic constraint is taken to be the Phillips curve:

$$\pi_t = a\pi_{t-1} - bu_t + c \qquad 3.19$$

where a is between zero and unity, and b and c are positive. This relationship describes current inflation as a function of both price expectations, as characterised by past inflation experience, and excess supply, as represented by the current unemployment rate. This gives a long-run Phillips curve that is steeper than the short-run Phillips curve. The problem then is to minimise J subject to Equation 3.19, which is a standard dynamic programming problem.[9] MacRae (1977) solves the model, and demonstrates that minimising Equation 3.17 subject to the long-run trade-off between π_t and u_t, derived from Equation 3.19 where $\pi_t = \pi_{t-1}$, would yield the long-run optimum welfare loss for the electorate, if the electoral period were infinite. He also shows that the economy displays turnpike behaviour, first moving towards the long-run optimum values of π and u, and then moving away as the planning horizon of the party in power shortens with the approaching election year. With a fixed electoral period this turnpike behaviour is repeated in every election period. The result is a limit cycle in u_t and π_t, if the economy is stable, i.e. if a < 1, with inflation always greater than the long-run optimum. Finally, MacRae shows that if the electorate votes strategically then the government can be induced to promote the public interest while being held accountable through periodic elections.

Another major contributor to modern PBC theory has been Frey. He has produced a number of useful survey works, e.g. Frey (1978a, b and c), and has made a number of significant contributions to the development of the PBC theory, with a number of associates.[10] Perhaps his major contribution has been to draw attention to the fact that the government's utility is unlikely to depend solely on its vote share, but may depend also on ideological factors. Such factors had been ignored by Nordhaus and MacRae, who had implicitly adopted the median voter theorem (MVT)[11] in their analysis of a two-party system. The MVT is related to the work of Hotelling (1929), whose spatial competition model of duopoly should be familiar to many students. The idea was that the two firms (duopolists) would locate centrally in the available space. Hotelling noted that, in principle, the argument had many applications and that it could be applied to political competition, with two parties replacing the two firms. The two parties would then be expected to choose policies in the centre of the political space in order to try to attract the vote of the median voter, and have the widest political appeal. In a truly political system it would be expected, even in the two-party case, that each party would have loyal supporters, i.e. voters, members, campaigners and financial backers. These supporters will have to be satisfied if the party is to survive. Thus an ideology is imposed on the party. This constrains the political programme that it can offer in trying to attract the floating, or uncommitted, votes necessary to top up its support by the faithful in order to achieve electoral success. Thus each party, including the incumbent, is likely to have ideological, as well as electoral, goals. Admittedly the ideological goals cannot be effectively pursued unless the party is in government. But, if the party is in power, and feels that it has sufficient popularity to be assured of re-election when the time comes, then ideological, e.g. redistribution of income, goals may be pursued.

Frey (1978b) suggests that if the popularity rating (POP_t) exceeds that judged to be necessary for re-election (POP_t^*), then ideological goals may be pursued. Conversely, if POP_t is less than POP_t^*, the policies must be adopted to improve popularity. POP_t may be gauged from opinion poll survey data and from any elections occurring within the term of office, e.g. local or by-elections in the UK, and congressional elections in the US, if POP_t relates to the popularity of the presidential administration. These election results would, however, have to be adjusted for particular local and special issues which might bias their usefulness as a measure of the popularity of the government. POP_t^* would be estimated on the basis of the desired electoral outcome and the electoral popularity cycle. The former encompasses the idea that a minority government might wish to increase its majority in the parliament, senate or congress in order to pursue its ideological objectives more effectively, and would require a larger POP_t^* than a simple re-election objective. The electoral popularity cycle relates to the observation that new administrations tend to experience a 'honeymoon' period, followed by a decline in popularity, and then an increase in popularity as the election approaches and the programme of the alternative administrations are critically evaluated. This is a well-documented international phenomenon (see Alt (1979, Ch. 6) for a summary of UK evidence). More commonly, however, in the US, it has been assumed that the President's popularity declines continuously from one election to the next, (see Frey and Schneider, 1978b, for example). The joint consideration of ideological and re-election objectives is likely to complicate models of political-economic interaction and to make PBC analysis more difficult, with the result that the regular cycle, implied by the (fixed) electoral period induced economic cycle argument, is unlikely to be observed.

There are a number of other factors that must also be considered in formulating a model of political-economic interaction which is capable of explaining real-world outcomes. First, the economic constraints faced by a government are likely to be far more complex than the simple inflation—unemployment trade-offs considered by Nordhaus and MacRae; a more detailed model of the economy is required. Secondly, there are likely to be additional constraints on the government's activity in the form of institutional and bureaucratic constraints, such as those imposed by the Civil Service and the Central Bank. Thirdly, the model needs to take account of how popularity or the vote share can be converted into numbers of seats held in the parliament, senate or congress. This will differ between the British first-past-the-post system, and a proportional representation system. Fourthly, the case of more than two parties and the concomitant possibility of coalitions must be allowed for in many countries. Fifthly, problems caused by a non-fixed electoral period must be tackled. In the UK, for example, the electoral date is chosen by the incumbant party and is, therefore, part of the political game. Lachler (1982) and Chappell and Peel (1979) have considered the effects on the PBC of treating the election date as endogenously determined, using models related to that of Nordhaus.

Other contributions to the theory of the PBC include those of Tufte (1974, 1978), who provides some evidence in favour of a PBC in disposable income, for the US in particular. He also considers the possibility that monetary policy has been used, along with other fiscal policy instruments, to generate the cycle in disposable income. Luckett and Potts (1980) examine critically the hypothesis that monetary policy has been used, for partisan reasons, to generate a cycle in disposable income. Frey (1978 a and c), among others, has also considered the existence of a PBC in the growth of disposable income.

From the previous discussion it can be concluded that the existence of a PBC has the following prerequisites: First, economic variables must influence voting behaviour, otherwise there would be no point in the government manipulating the economy in order to try to win votes. Studies of this underlying hypothesis (i.e. estimates of popularity or vote functions) are numerous, and a survey of some of the results is provided in the next chapter. It is sufficient to note, at this stage, that there is some evidence that economic variables affect political popularity but that there is no general agreement on which are the key economic variables, and there is a suggestion that the economic variables that most affect popularity change from time to time. Secondly, the government must be able to manipulate the target economic variables (i.e. those influencing its popularity) by judicious use of fiscal, monetary and other policy instruments. Because a number of the target variables are probably real variables, such as unemployment, this requires that fiscal and/or monetary policies can have real effects. There cannot be 100 per cent crowding-out and/or there is no monetary policy neutrality. Evidence pertaining to this underlying hypothesis relies on regressing policy instruments, such as the money supply or the level of government expenditure, on target variables. The estimated relationships are called policy reaction functions. They show how the government responds, by using its policy instruments, to changes in the target variables, under the assumption that the government believes that its policy responses will influence the target variables. (Estimates of policy reaction functions will also be considered in the next chapter.) At this stage, it is germane to note that policy reactions, to the target variables, have been found, but that there is no general agreement on which the relevant target variables are or on whether they are the same variables in different time periods.

Given the estimation of satisfactory popularity and policy reaction functions, the potential for cycle creation by the government seems to be evident. It remains to be proved conclusively that government has actually created an economic cycle. Any cycle created will be conditioned by whether the electoral period is fixed or variable, and by the assumption made regarding the electorate. Of particular importance are the assumptions that the electorate is myopic and that they form expectations of inflation adaptively. Nordhaus and MacRae have demonstrated that, with a fixed electoral period and a myopic electorate which forms inflationary expectations adaptively, a regular cycle in inflation and unemployment can be generated. It is interesting to speculate whether a business cycle, howbeit irregular, could still be generated in the absence of these assumptions. Evidence pertaining to these issues, and concerning the existence of a PBC, will be discussed in the next chapter.

Finally, to conclude this section, some consideration should be given to the implications of our discussion of the modern PBC theory for the role of the government in the cycle. It has been noted that, with a myopic electorate, a cycle can be created. Minford and Peel (1982), however, have considered the case of two political parties, each with a loyal set of voters and where there is a set of floating voters. The latter are endowed with rationally formed expectations and vote, accordingly, for the party which offers the best menu of policy, on the basis of expected future performance. Using this model they estimate policy reaction and popularity functions for each party and discover party political differences. Conservative governments react more to inflation, to which their stock of voters are assumed to be more averse, and Labour governments react more to unemployment, for similar reasons. As a result, Labour governments have a more lax money supply policy and larger budget deficits than Conservative governments. Their results will be discussed further in the next chapter. No theory of cyclical development of the economy is presented by Minford and Peel. Neither is there any theory developed to explain government change, which could explain an economic cycle in terms of alternating policies. Their theory does, however, try to merge political-economic considerations with the REH. What seems to be required is a model in which the government pursues its ideological and re-election objectives subject to economic, institutional and bureaucratic constraints. The other economic agents should be assumed to have their own objective functions and should be endowed with rationally formed expectations, as a first approximation. The government could, therefore, not take the economic constraints as fixed in formulating the optimal policy response, designed to achieve its objectives. It would be involved in playing a political game against a reactive economic environment, rather than against nature, as well as against other political parties. It may be the case that, even under the REH, the government, or alternations in the political persuasion of the party in power, could create an electorally-induced economic cycle. This remains to be demonstrated for an electorate endowed with rationally formed expectations of future economic outcomes, although its possibility has been demonstrated under the assumption of a myopic electorate. The general implications of modern PBC theory is, however, that the government actually creates an economic cycle, within the electoral period, in pursuit of its own objectives. This contrasts with traditional Keynesian policy analysis which assumes that the objective of government policy is to maximise general economic welfare and that this can be assisted by undertaking active anti-cyclical policy. The further consideration that the government pursues ideological goals, in addition to re-election goals, introduces the possibility of an economic cycle generated by alternating governments with different ideologies. This cycle would be of a longer period than the within-electoral-period cycles considered by Nordhaus and MacRae, but would still be, to some extent, conditioned by the electoral period.

3.4 SUMMARY AND CONCLUSIONS

Both the EBC and PBC theories seem to indicate a need for careful consideration of the role of the government in cycle generation and attenuation. The former, as a result of the REH and the Lucas (1976) critique of policy analysis, suggests that policy analysis will be complicated and should involve game theoretic considerations requiring the specification of a government objective function or a set of alternative government strategies. The PBC theory gives the government a clear role in business cycle generation, but the myopic behaviour imputed to the electorate is perhaps dubious. The challenge is to derive a PBC theory in which the government pursues its objectives, ideological and re-elective, subject to economic, bureaucratic and institutional constraints, in which the other agents are endowed with rationally formed expectations and pursue their own objectives. This would also indicate that a game theoretic formulation was required. Thus both theories imply that, in order to endogenise the government in cycle models, it is not sufficient simply to give the government and objective of maximising welfare in general or simply to constrain its policy choices by invoking a government budget equation. The government should instead be treated as having its own objectives to maximise, in a constrained optimisation problem, and it should be observed that these objectives may well conflict with those of some of the other economic agents.

It is to be noted, however, that the role of the government in the EBC and the modern PBC theories, so far formulated, is very different. The EBC theory gives the government no real role in cycle generation, except to the extent that it may contribute to the cycle by adding monetary shocks to the other shocks hitting the economy. But the other shocks would probably generate a cycle anyway. No role is envisaged for active monetary stabilisation policy. In the modern PBC theory the government actively creates the cycle, and has the capability of doing so using its monetary and fiscal policy instruments. The cycle so created is not caused by economic policy mismanagement: resulting from the long and variable lags in the effects of monetary policy, postulated in Friedman (1974); or due to policy reactions in the wrong stage of the cycle, as discussed in Bronfenbrenner (ed.) 1969); or even resulting from stop—go policies, see Mathews (1969).

Some of the evidence concerning the modern cycle theories, and their underlying hypotheses, will be reviewed in the next chapter.

4 Tests of the Modern Cycle Theories and their Underlying Hypotheses

4.1 INTRODUCTION

There have been few direct tests of the modern EBC and PBC theories. This is largely because complete econometric models, representing these theories, have not yet been developed. It is usually the implications of the theories, or their underlying hypotheses, that are tested. A notable exception is the attempt by Kydland and Prescott (1982) to estimate some of the parameters of an EBC model, on the basis of empirical observations on a number of economic variables and informed guestimates of the parameter values connected with the rest of the economic variables. McCallum (1978) tests the time series implications of the PBC and EBC theories and finds that the data favour the EBC formulation. Also, Nordhaus (1975) and MacRae (1977) present some results pertaining to their PBC theories. The rest of the tests considered in this chapter are concerned with the underlying hypotheses of the PBC and EBC theories.

The EBC theory relies on the REH and the NRH, or the structural neutrality hypothesis (SNH),[1] and implies, given continuous market clearing, that anticipated changes in the money supply have no effects on real economic variables. Direct tests of the latter proposition, such as those presented in Barro (1977, 1978), can be viewed as tests of the joint RE—SN hypothesis, as Leiderman (1980) points out. Leiderman observes that the REH can be an important source of overidentifying restrictions[2] and that the SN hypothesis imposes additional restrictions. He also shows that the restrictions implied by the RE and SN hypotheses can be tested separately in a nested testing procedure.[3]

The modern PBC theory relies on certain linkages between the economy and the polity on the assumption that the government can utilise monetary and fiscal, and perhaps other (e.g. incomes) policies to influence real, as well as nominal, variables, and on the myopic behaviour of the electorate. If it is granted that it can be accepted that the government can manipulate the economy to achieve its goals – a proposition that might be disputed by a new classical economist who believed in zero fiscal multiplier effects; and if, further, it could be demonstrated that popularity, or votes, were significantly influenced by economic variables and that government policy instruments react to those variables which the popularity function indicates most affect popularity, or votes, then there is a basis for the proposition that the government might manipulate the economy to win elections. Whether or not it would attempt to do so would depend on its objective function. Another key hypothesis in the modern PBC models of Nordhaus and MacRae is that the electorate is myopic.

In Section 4.2 tests of the hypothesis that only unanticipated changes in the money supply affect real variables are discussed. These are implicitly tests of the joint RE—SN hypothesis and also in this section tests of the separate underlying, RE and SN, hypotheses are considered. In Section 4.3 various estimates of the popularity and policy reaction functions are discussed. Section 4.4 will consider McCallum's (1978) comparison of the implications of the EBC and PBC theories. It will also discuss the tests performed by Nordhaus and MacRae of their theories. In the case of MacRae's work this involves considera-tion of whether the electorate have behaved myopically in the US. A parallel analysis of the electorate's behaviour, undertaken by Alt (1979) in the UK, is also discussed. In Section 4.4, the estimates derived by Kydland and Prescott (1982) for their EBC model will be considered. Finally, Section 4.5 will provide a summary and draw some conclusions.

4.2 TESTS OF THE RATIONAL EXPECTATIONS (RE) AND STRUCTURAL NEUTRALITY (SN) HYPOTHESES

Perhaps the best-known tests of the joint RE—SN hypotheses are those performed by Barro (1977, 1978). In these papers Barro used annual data on the US economy to test for the relative influence of anticipated and unanticipated monetary growth on unemployment, prices and output. The original analysis did not employ a simultaneous equation estimation technique, but relied instead upon OLS[4] estimates of the various equations. Barro and Rush (1980) update the analysis and confirm the results using a simultaneous equation estimation technique. They also rework the analysis using quarterly data and again confirm the main findings. The major conclusion, arising out of Barro's (1977, 1978) papers was that unanticipated, rather than anticipated, monetary growth affected the real variables under consideration, output and unemployment, and that, perhaps surprisingly, the price equation was unsatisfactory. In this section the tests of the influence of monetary growth on output performed in Barro (1978) will largely be concentrated upon.

It will be recalled from Chapter 3 that the output equation can be written as follows, if a lagged dependent variable is included as an explanatory variable:

$$y_t = y'_{nt} + \alpha \sum_{i=0}^{\infty} \beta^i (p_{t-i} - p^*_{t-i}) + \sum_{i=0}^{\infty} \beta^i \varepsilon_{t-i} \qquad 4.1$$

where y_t is the $\log_e$ of output at time t, y'_{nt} is a transformation of its natural rate,[5] p_{t-i} is the $\log_e$ of the price level at time $t-i$, and p^*_{t-i} is its rational expectation, and ε_t is a random error term at time t, representing other, perhaps real, shocks to output.

If it is assumed that the money supply and the price level are closely related, in accordance with monetarist propostitions, then Equation 4.1 can be written as follows:

$$y_t = y''_{nt} + \sum_{i=0}^{\infty} \gamma^i (m_{t-i} - m^*_{t-i}) + \sum_{i=0}^{\infty} \psi^i e_{1t-i} \qquad 4.2$$

where the parameters will differ from those of Equation 4.1 after replacing p_{t-i} with m_{t-i}, and so will the parameters in the process generating y'_{nt}, now denoted y''_{nt}, and e_{1t} is an (assumed random) error process incorporating the errors resulting from the substitution of m_{t-i} for p_{t-i}.

The procedure proposed by Barro for testing the neutrality of money is to compare an equation like 4.2 with an equation like 4.3 below, which includes anticipated monetary variables as well as unanticipated monetary variables. The aim is to test whether the parameters on the anticipated monetary variables are significantly different from zero. An F test was used by Barro.

$$y_t = y''_{nt} + \sum_{i=0}^{\infty} \gamma^i(m_{t-i} - m^*_{t-i}) + \sum_{i=0}^{\infty} \eta^i m^*_{t-i} + \sum_{i=0}^{\infty} \psi^i e_{1t-i} \qquad 4.3$$

In this case the null hypothesis in the test would be that $\eta = 0$, i.e. H_0: $\eta = 0$, since then $\eta^i = 0$ for all i. The test cannot, however, be performed by estimating Equations 4.2 and 4.3 and seeing if the addition of the m^*_{t-i} terms contributed significantly to the explanation of y_t, using an F test. This is because Equations 4.2 and 4.3 are not directly estimable. The reasons for this are: that y''_{nt} and m^*_{t-i} are not directly observable; and that there is an infinite distributed lag process on both e_{1t} and $(m_t - m^*_t)$, which means that there will be insufficient observations to estimate the equations directly. The implied geometric lag structure could, however, be utilised to simplify the equations and make them estimable, if the problem of the unobservable variables could be dealt with.[6] If the implied geometric lag structure is ignored, however, there will be an acute degree of freedom problem because there will be an infinite number of parameters, η_i, ψ_i, γ_i, $i=1,...,\infty$, to estimate from a finite number of observations. In this case approximations to Equations 4.2 and 4.3 must be considered.

Barro (1978) suggests a fairly *ad hoc* process for explaining y''_{nt}, which is, however, more sophisticated than the more common assumption that y_{nt} follows a (log) linear trend.[7] The problems implied by the error process $\sum_{i=0}^{\infty} \psi^i e_{1t-i}$ are ignored by assuming that this process is random, which shall be denoted by ε_{1t}. Barro estimates the model using unanticipated monetary growth $(\Delta m_{t-i} - \Delta m^*_{t-i})$, rather than unanticipated levels of the money supply $(m_{t-i} - m^*_{t-i})$.[8] Thus, an explanation of the unobservable variable Δm^*_t rather than one of m^*_t is required. An *ad hoc* equation, which is a crude combination of a policy reaction function and a government budget equation, is postulated for explaining Δm_t. The estimated regression parameters are then used, along with the observations on the explanatory variables, to generate Δm_t^* and the same equation can be used to derive Δm_{t-i}^*. Given the fairly poor fit of the Δm_t equation, estimated by Barro, the unanticipated monetary growth variables $(\Delta m_{t-i} - \Delta m_{t-i}^*)$ were rather large. The remaining problem, in approximating Equations 4.2 and 4.3, was to decide on the number of lagged terms to include, i.e. the maximal size of i. After empirical experimentation with a number of i's, Barro chose i=3. His final output equation was therefore:

$$y_t = y_{nt}'' + \sum_{i=0}^{3} a_i (\Delta m_{t-i} - \Delta m_{t-i}^*) + \varepsilon_{1t} \qquad 4.4$$

where

$$y_{nt}'' = a_4 + a_5 MIL_t + a_6 t \qquad 4.5$$

and a_4 is a constant, MIL_t is a military personnel (draft pressure) variable[9], and t is a time trend. The equation for Δm_t^* was:

$$\Delta m_t^* = \alpha_5 + \sum_{i=1}^{2} \alpha_i \Delta m_{t-i} + \alpha_3 FEDV_t + \alpha_4 UN_{t-1} \qquad 4.6$$

so that:

$$\Delta m_t = \Delta m_t^* + \varepsilon_{2t}$$

where ε_{2t} is the random error process in the money growth equation; $FEDV_t = \log_e (FED_t) - [\log_e (FED_t)]_t^*$; FED_t is the current level of real federal expenditures and $[\log(FED)]_t^*$ is an exponentially declining distributed lag of current and past values of $\log(FED)$; and $UN \equiv \log_e [(U/1-U)]$ where U is the unemployment rate in the total labour force. UN is a cyclical variable and FEDV measures federal expenditure relative to 'normal'.

This model was tested against a similar model with the output equation (4.4) replaced by (4.7):

$$y_t = y_{nt}'' + \sum_{i=0}^{3} a_i (\Delta m_{t-i} - \Delta m_{t-i}^*) + \sum_{i=0}^{3} b_i m_{t-i}^* + \varepsilon_{3t} \qquad 4.7$$

An F test supported the H_0: $b_0 = b_1 = b_2 = b_3 = 0$, implying that unanticipated monetary growth, rather than anticipated monetary growth, influences ouput.

The proportion of the variation in the growth of the money supply, explained by the model, was only 77 per cent, so that the unanticipated monetary growth terms were rather large. Another feature of Barro's results was the finding that $a_1 > a_0 >$

$a_2 > a_3$, so that the estimated coefficients on the lagged monetary growth terms have an inverted V, or humped, structure. Also the error process ($\hat{\varepsilon}_{1t}$) was clear from first order autocorrelation (AR(1)) according to the calculated Durbin h-statistic. Hence, neither the infinite moving average on the error process, which can under certain conditions be converted to an AR(1) process, nor the infinite geometrically declining weights, which are implicit in the derivation of the Lucas supply hypothesis, which is claimed by Barro to underlie his model, were evident.

Similar studies to those of Barro were undertaken by Bellante et al. (1982) and Attfield et al. (1981a and b) for the UK. The former study finds that Barro's money growth equation is directly applicable to the UK ($R^2 = 0.68$), in the post-war period, and that only unanticipated monetary growth has real effects on unemployment and output. Anticipated monetary growth, it was found, did not add significantly to the explanatory power of the equations, including unanticipated monetary growth, explaining output and unemployment. Thus the results support Barro's results for the US. Attfield et al.'s (1981b) paper deals with annual data, while their (1981a) paper uses quarterly data, therefore this chapter will concentrate on the annual data study in order to make comparison's with Barro's (1978) findings. Their approach was very similar to Barro's. They do, however, use a simultaneous equation (maximum likelihood) estimator, but they find that the output and money growth equation estimates are similar, whether OLS or the maximum likelihood estimator are used. Their results are also similar: the error process on the output equation is judged to be devoid of AR(1), the parameters on the lagged monetary variables demonstrate a humped shape, and the monetary growth equation has a rather poor ($R^2 = 0.68$) explanatory power and is *ad hoc,* as is the equation explaining y''_{nt}. Most importantly, again using the equivalent of an F test,[10] they accept the joint hypothesis, when the probability of a type I error (α) is set at 2½ per cent, that the parameters on the anticipated monetary growth variables, when they are included in an output equation along with the unanticipated monetary growth variables, are zero.

Leiderman (1980) shows how the RE and SN assumptions,

implicitly jointly tested by Barro (1977) in his examination of
the effect of anticipated and unanticipated monetary growth on
unemployment, can be tested separately in a nested testing
procedure.[11] Leiderman derives the restrictions on Barro's
(1977) model implicit in the REH and SNH; he then estimates
three versions of Barro's model, an unrestricted model (UM), a
model subject to the derived RE restrictions (REM), and a
model subject to the joint RE and SN restrictions (RESNM). A
likelihood ratio (LR) test of the REM against the UM shows
that the RE restrictions can be accepted, and an LR test of the
RESNM against the REM shows that the SN restrictions can
be accepted. SN cannot be tested independently of some
assumption about expectations formation and must, therefore,
be tested in this nested manner. It could only be tested in
connection with an acceptance of the expectations formation
hypothesis. If the RE restrictions had been rejected, then no test
for SN could have been made unless an alternative set of
restrictions, derived from some other expectations formation
mechanism, could be found and tested and accepted. A truly
nested testing procedure can only proceed as far as the last
acceptable nested hypothesis. Driscoll *et al.* (1983b) have
shown that, in this case, the test for RE and SN is invalid. They
note that the so-called unrestricted model (UM) is not the
unrestricted reduced form model (URFM). The UM includes
various exclusion restrictions (i.e. zero parameter restrictions)
when compared with the URFM. An LR test of the UM against
the URFM shows that these exclusion restrictions are unaccept-
able. The UM is thus not correctly parameterised, and the test
of the RE and SN restrictions based on it are not truly nested
and are, therefore, of dubious validity. Additionally, it is shown
that a better fitting money equation can be derived from Barro's
(1977) data set and that the joint RESN restrictions, derived
from the reformulated model, cannot be accepted.

    Driscoll *et al.* (1983a) have utilised Leiderman's suggested
procedure to test separately for the RE and SN hypotheses in
the UK; and Driscoll *et al.* (1981a) examine Attfield *et al.'s*
(1981a) model more closely using Leiderman's suggested
approach. In examining Attfield *et al.'s* work they concur that
the joint RESN hypothesis can be accepted when α is set at 2½
per cent. Attfield *et al.* noted that the joint RESN hypothesis

could be rejected when α is set at 1 per cent, and they also report that RESN restrictions in Barro's (1977) model, which they re-estimated, can be accepted when α is set at 2½ per cent, but they must be rejected when α is set at 1 per cent. Testing for RE and SN separately, using the same data set as *Attfield et al.,* Driscoll *et al.* (1981a) find that the RE restrictions cannot be rejected when α is set at 1 per cent, but can be rejected when α is set at 5 per cent. Only if the RE restrictions are accepted, on this basis, can the SN restrictions be validly tested using the nested testing procedure. The test for the SN restrictions shows that they can be accepted for $\alpha = 5$ per cent. Thus it can be concluded that the rather unsatisfactory conclusion, that the joint RESN hypothesis can be accepted when $\alpha = 2½$ per cent, and rejected when $\alpha = 1$ per cent, derived in Attfield *et al.'s* paper, is the result of similar uncertainty regarding the acceptability of the RE restrictions in their model.

Driscoll *et al.* (1983a) derive an alternative model, based on log levels rather than on log differences, of the money supply. The aim was to derive a model more directly consistent with the Lucas supply hypothesis which was postulated in terms of log levels,[12] (see Chapter 3). The results of the study, which employed post-war annual data, were that the equation explaining the ($\log_e$) money supply had a very good fit ($R^2 = 99$ per cent), as did the unrestricted model as a whole, and that the RE and the joint RESN restrictions could not be accepted. Although a good fit, the UM could not be tested against the URFM because of the lack of degrees of freedom. An alternative, more direct approach to testing these models for RE and SN restrictions is explored by Driscoll *et al.* (1981b). They work directly with the autoregressive form of the supply hypothesis, i.e. the form with the lagged dependent variable (see equation 3.5) and replace p_t with m_t, rather than its moving average representation, (i.e. equation 4.2). This saves significantly on degrees of freedom and avoids the need to approximate the moving average process on the monetary shocks. Again, a reasonably good fitting model is derived, with a good explanation of the $\log_e$ level of the money supply ($R^2 = 99$ per cent) and again the RE and joint RESN restrictions on the model are rejected. With this formulation it is possible to test for the UM, against the URFM, and the likelihood ratio test indicates that the restrictions implicit in the UM can be accepted.

The conclusions to be derived from these empirical studies are that with some sets of *ad hoc* equations the RE and SN hypotheses can be accepted and with other sets they can be rejected. The major differences in the results seem to be derived as a result of the specification of the money supply generating process. This is usually an *ad hoc* mixture of a government budget equation and a policy reaction function. The studies that formulate the model in terms of monetary growth achieve a poorer fit than those utilising the $\log_e$ level of the money supply, which are more consistent with the Lucas supply hypothesis, discussed in Chapter 3. The monetary shocks derived in the former models will be correspondingly larger than those derived in the latter models. This may perhaps account for the reduced explanatory power of the monetary shocks in the $\log_e$ level formulations and, therefore, also for the different results derived from the testing of the RE and SN restrictions.

Alternative approaches to the testing of the natural rate hypothesis are reviewed in Barro (1981, Ch. 2), and Pesaran (1982) gives a critique of various proposed tests of the joint RE and natural rate hypotheses.

4.3 ESTIMATES OF POPULARITY AND POLICY REACTION FUNCTIONS

(a) Popularity functions
A popularity function is an equation relating votes cast or popularity ratings, derived from opinion poll survey data, to economic variables.

Much of the original empirical work was undertaken in the US. This work tended to concentrate on the analysis of voting behaviour, at either presidential or congressional elections, rather than opinion poll survey data. Kramer (1971) found evidence that real personal income had a significant influence on congressional elections. Stigler (1973) casts doubt on Kramer's findings. Lepper (1974) finds evidence of voters' aversion to increases in unemployment and to changes (in either direction) in prices. Also concentrating on congressional elections, Arcelus and Meltzer (1975a) find that, with the possible exception of inflation, aggregate economic variables do not affect the election outcome. In the discussion of the latter paper various other studies, supportive and unsupportive of the hypothesis that voting behaviour is influenced by aggregate economic variables, are cited. Fair (1978) examines the effects of economic events on voters for the President. Fair finds that economic events, as measured by the change in real economic activity in the year of the election, do appear to have an important effect on votes for the President. It does not matter much whether this change is measured by the growth rate of real *per capita* GNP or by the change in the unemployment rate. Other measures of economic performance added little to the explanation of the President's vote share. Additionally, voters were found to attach a very high (probably infinite) discount rate on past economic events. Thus they concentrate on current, election year, economic events in making their voting decisions and, therefore, display myopic behaviour. Frey and Schneider (1978b) estimate both policy reaction and popularity functions for the US. They use Gallup poll opinion survey data on whether those polled approve or disapprove of the job being done by the President. They find that the unemployment and inflation rates, as well as the rate of growth of consumption, significantly influence presidential popularity.

Complementary studies have been undertaken in the UK. Goodhart and Bhansali (1970) found inflation and unemployment to have significant influences on the government's popularity lead, and the popularity of the government and the opposition parties using opinion poll survey data. Frey and Garbers (1971) contest these results on statistical grounds. Miller and Mackie (1973) find that electoral popularity cycles,[13] represented by dummy variables, can explain the cycles in the popularity data and that aggregate economic variables do not add significantly to the explanatory power of their model. Frey and Schneider (1978a) find that the popularity lead of the government is significantly influenced by inflation, unemployment and real disposable income, even when election popularity cycle dummy variables are included. Alt (1979, Ch. 6) discusses Frey and Schneider's, and other evidence on the influence of economic variables on government support, and Chrystal and Alt (1981a) also discuss Frey and Schneider's results. They argue that only the growth of real disposable income influences popularity – Frey and Schneider's findings of significant influences of inflation and unemployment being the result of factors peculiar to their data period. Frey and Schneider (1981, 1982), however, provide an updated version of their original equation, again confirming the influence of inflation and unemployment on government popularity.

With regard to Chrystal and Alt's finding, that the influences of inflation and unemployment on popularity are unstable, Mosley (1978) has postulated a model based upon satisfying behaviour[14] by the electorate. He builds a model, related to that of Nordhaus (1975), in which it is assumed that voters' preferences are believed by the political parties to be subject to periodic shifts in the weights attached to unemployment and inflation in their vote functions. In Mosley's model the voter is not, as in Nordhaus's, assumed to be myopic with respect to past economic outcomes but is instead assumed to pursue satisficing behaviour. The voters' order of priorities – between inflation and unemployment – are thus viewed as being fixed for a period and then as displaying discrete changes as a result of the variables crossing a threshold at which social and economic insecurities are triggered off. In his model the trigger levels on unemployment and inflation occur when unemployment and inflation exceed their current trend values so that inflation or unemployment reach crisis levels. It is these shifts in the weights attached to inflation and unemployment in the votes function that elicit responses from the government and generate a political business cycle in these variables. Mosley (1978) presents evidence to support his thesis that the votes function swivels between inflation and unemployment crisis periods. He also finds some support for the hypothesis, also borne out in Goodhart and Bhansali's (1970) study, that Labour governments are on the whole more responsive to movements in the unemployment rate, and less sensitive to movements in the inflation rate, than Conservative governments. Finally, he finds that given combinations of inflation and unemployment imply a progressively smaller penalty at the polls as time progresses.

Chrystal and Alt (1981a) review Mosley's finding, as well as those of Frey and Schneider (1978). Pissarides (1980) finds that the percentage growth in consumption, the tax ratio, and the unemployment and inflation rates have significant influences on the government popularity lead even if electoral popularity cycle dummy variables are included. Finally, Borooah and Van der Ploeg (1982) provide evidence for the UK that the criteria for economic success changes significantly over time. This, they note, gives some insight into the apparent instability of voting and popularity functions found previously in the literature, e.g. by Stigler (1973) and Arcelus and Meltzer (1975a) in the US, and by Mosley (1978) and Chrystal and Alt (1981a) in the UK. The economic variables found to be significant in the Borooah and Van der Ploeg study, were the levels and changes in the inflation and unemployment rates, and the rate of growth of real disposable income and the change in this rate of growth. Their relative significance varied in the three sub-periods studied and additionally, in one sub-period, the balance of payments exerted a significant influence on the government popularity lead, and in another the tax burden exerted a significant influence.

Frey and Schneider (1978c) and Schneider *et al.* (1981) have undertaken studies for countries other than the UK and the US; and Tufte (1978) has collected evidence from a number of countries on the effects of economic outcomes on political popularity.

The broad conclusion arising out of these various empirical studies, of the influence of economic variables on popularity, seems to be that economic variables do significantly affect popularity, at least in some time periods. There is, however, no general agreement on which economic variables are most influential and there is a strong suggestion that different economic variables affect popularity to different degrees at different times. Perhaps the clearest indications of this latter observation are the switches in the ranking of unemployment and inflation as the economic factor of most concern to the electorate recorded in opinion poll surveys in the 1970s and early 1980s.

(b) Policy reaction functions
A policy reaction function is a relationship between a government policy instrument and target economic variables. The target variables may well be the economic variables that most influence popularity but may also be ideological economic

variables, such as the distribution of income.

A major contribution to the analysis of policy reaction functions in the US was that of Friedlaender (1973). An attempt was made to determine the weights attached to various macro-policy goals during the Eisenhower and Kennedy—Johnson administrations. The government was assumed to maximise a quadratic objective function subject to economic constraints expressed by the MIT—FRB econometric model. Each of the policy variables was regressed on a number of potential policy target variables and slope and intercept dummy variables were included in an attempt to capture the effects that the particular administration had on the estimated coefficients. The reduced form coefficients of the estimated MIT—FRB model were then used to determine the weights, by combining these estimated reduced form coefficients, with those derived from the policy reaction functions, using equations relating these coefficients to the weights derived from consideration of the optimisation problem. It was found that both the Eisenhower and Kennedy—Johnson administrations placed more weight on price stability and on a favourable balance of payments than on full employment, but that the Kennedy—Johnson administration placed relatively more weight on full employment and on the trade balance than did the Eisenhower administration.

Fisher (1968, 1970) analyses fairly *ad hoc* monetary policy reaction functions for the UK, justifying his approach by reference to Reuber (1964) and Dewald and Johnson (1963). The instruments considered were the liquid assets ratio, the Treasury bill rate, the 2½ per cent consol rate, the bank rate, the level of special deposits, and hire purchase conditions. The target variables considered were foreign currency reserves, unemployment and inflation. A trade-off between the unemployment objective on the one hand and the inflation and foreign currency reserve objectives on the other, is discovered, and the three formal instruments, bank rate, special deposits, and hire purchase controls, show generally firm and consistent relations to objectives.

Pissarides (1972) provides a study for the UK that is more comparable, methodologically, to that of Friedlaender (1973). Again the problem of maximising a quadratic objective function subject to a reduced form economic model is considered.

Relationships between the weights and the estimated coefficients of the policy reaction and the reduced form economic model are derived. Then the estimated coefficients are used to calculate the weights. The form of the reaction function is derived from consideration of the optimisation problem, but the reduced form economic model is specified in an *ad hoc* manner. Rather than use an existing model, Pissarides (1972) simply regresses the targets on the instruments and uses the estimated parameters in his derivation of the weights. The instruments considered were the bank rate, hire purchase controls and the tax rate, and the objectives were assumed to be the level of foreign currency reserves, unemployment and the price level. The most significant result to emerge from this study was that the authorities were willing on average to change their instruments by up to 40 per cent of their level (quarterly) in order to eliminate unfavourable forces acting on the objectives, but were very unwilling to exceed this limit, with bigger concessions being made for reserves and unemployment than for inflation.

More recent estimates of the policy reaction function in the US and the UK have been made by Frey and Schneider (1978a and b). For the UK they consider the instruments: real government expenditure on consumption and investment, subsidies to enterprise, grants to the personal sector, and real total government tax receipts. These are regressed on the difference between the popularity lead and that deemed necessary for re-election. If the lead is insufficient then expansionary policy dominates; if it is sufficient then ideological goals dominate. The two parties are assumed to have different ideological goals. In addition various economic constraints, such as the balance of payments, the real wage rate and the unemployment rate, influence the policy variables. All these factors are incorporated in an equation involving a number of dummy variables and good statistical fits are derived for the policy reaction functions estimated. Their results are updated for the UK in Frey and Schneider (1981a). A similar methodology guides their analysis of US data. The instruments considered are non-defence government expenditure, government transfers to private households and the number of civilian government jobs, and fits the data reasonably well. Frey and Schneider (1978c) and Schneider *et al.* (1981) perform similar analyses for other countries.

Chrystal and Alt (1981a and b) have perhaps been most critical of Frey and Schneider's estimates of the policy reaction function, at least for the UK. They also offer an alternative explanation of government consumption expenditures, in the UK, based on the permanent income hypothesis.[15]

Additionally, there is mounting evidence, in the UK, that different governments have been differently sensitive to unemployment and inflation, and that the policy functions of the Labour and Conservative parties show that they respond differently to unemployment and inflation. Alt (1979, Ch. 7) has examined some of this evidence. More recently Minford and Peel (1982) have argued that, if it can be assumed that each of the two major parties has a stock of loyal supporters and that there is a stock of floating voters, then Conservative governments will have less inflationary policy targets, and stabilise inflation more and real incomes less, than Labour governments. This hypothesis is supported by their empirical results. Hibbs (1977) also examines evidence on whether macroeconomic policy differs between political parties. He analyses data from a number of countries which suggest that countries with socialist governments tend to have higher inflation and lower unemployment than those with Conservative governments. A more detailed analysis of the US and the UK, aimed at determining whether there are any significant differences in the unemployment rate series under, respectively, Conservative and Labour and Republican and Democratic regimes, is also undertaken by Hibbs. The results were broadly supportive of the hypothesis that, other things being equal, there would be a downward movement in the unemployment rate during the tenure of Democratic and Labour administrations and an upward movement in the unemployment rate during periods of Republican and Conservative rule in the US and the UK, respectively. Tufte (1978, Ch. 4) also reviews evidence on political parties and macroeconomic outcomes, concentrating mainly on evidence from the US. Given this accumulated evidence it is clear that in estimating policy reaction functions, and in formulating theories of the political business cycle, it is necessary to take account of the fact that governments respond differently to various economic variables, e.g. unemployment and inflation.

Due account should, therefore, be taken of ideological influences on government behaviour.

A major flaw in most of the work on policy reaction functions is that it does not acknowledge that the reaction function should be derived from a model in which government tries to maximise an objective function subject to the economic environment. Those sudies that do acknowledge this formally (e.g. Friedlaender, 1973, and Pissarides, 1972) consider very simple objective functions and, with the possible exception of Friedlaender, use unrealistically simple economic constraints. The complications arising out of the assumption that economic agents form expectations Muth-rationally have not been seriously tackled. Chow (1981) discusses the issues involved in control theoretic analysis under rational expectations and a number of related issues. The implication of his discussion is that a game theoretic model is required for the estimation of the government's and the public's reaction functions once RE is assumed. The reason for the complications lies in the fact that, under RE, the government cannot assume that the parameters of the economic constraints will remain constant if it changes its policy. The rational agents will be expected to respond to its policy initiative and will be assumed to know that the government knows that it is no longer playing a game against nature in the form of a fixed set of economic constraints. All the attributes requiring a game theoretic formulation are, therefore, present once rational expectations formation is assumed. One further shortcoming of the existing estimates of policy reaction functions is that they are usually estimated separately, by OLS, rather than simul-taneously with the assumed economic model.

A general conclusion can be drawn, from the review of estimated policy reaction functions despite their shortcomings, that policy instruments do seem to be related to hypothesised targets. There is, however, no general agreement on which are the major instruments or targets or on whether the relationships are stable over time. There is suggestive evidence, however, that policy reactions differ between political parties. Also one would expect there to be shifts in the policy reaction functions if there were shifts in the ranking of variables in popularity functions, as discussed in the previous sub-section.

4.4 TESTS OF THE EBC AND PBC THEORIES AND THEIR IMPLICATIONS

McCallum (1978) has tested the hypothesis that the addition of a dummy variable, descriptive of the phase of the electoral cycle to an autoregressive equation explaining unemployment, based on the Lucas supply hypothesis, should significantly increase the explanatory power of that equation if there is any truth in the PBC theory of Nordhaus (1975). Various electoral dummy variables are used and none is found significantly to improve the explanatory power of the autoregressive unemployment equation. The explanation of the unemployment rate, derived from the autoregressive equation, is fairly good, and, because it is based on the Lucas supply hypothesis, provides evidence supportive of that hypothesis.

Nordhaus (1975) tested implications of his PBC theory – that there will be high unemployment and deflation in the early years of the election period followed by an inflationary boom as the elections approach – by testing the hypothesis that the unemployment rate will rise in the first half, and fall in the second half, of the election period. The hypothesis is tested for the post-war period using data from a number of countries. For the US the hypothesis is supported for three of the election periods and rejected for two of them. In the two rejected, however, the incumbent party lost the election. The UK results are less supportive. Nordhaus postulates that this might be because the balance of payments constraint in the UK economy might have swamped the political cycle effects in the period under consideration.

Lachler (1978) argues that the target policy variable in the Nordhaus (1975) model might be considered to be inflation rather than employment. Solving for the cycle in inflation, he derives the alternative hypothesis that inflation should rise in the first half of the election period, and fall in the second half. He finds some support for this hypothesis using US data for the 1902—54 period, when counter-clockwise loops[16] were observed around the Phillips curve, and for Nordhaus's hypothesis for the 1954—72 period, when clockwise loops around the Phillips curve were observed.

MacRae (1977) argues that for a PBC to be generated the

government must believe that the electorate votes myopically, rather than strategically. He tests this hypothesis indirectly by estimating his model, in various election periods, using unemployment equations derived from both the strategic and the myopic voting hypotheses. The test is effected by seeing, administration by administration, whether the strategic or the myopic hypothesis did a better job of explaining actual recorded unemployment. MacRae finds that myopic hypothesis wins in the Kennedy—Johnson and the Johnson administrations, and that the strategic hypothesis wins in the second Eisenhower and the Nixon administrations. In no case is the better hypothesis inferior to the naive model, postulating no change in unemployment. The absolute level of explanatory power is found to be lower in Republican than Democratic periods. MacRae (1981) updates the evidence and finds it to be less supportive than his earlier study indicated of the myopic voting hypothesis and, therefore, of the PBC theory.

Alt (1979, Ch. 7) adopts the MacRae model and testing methodology in order to test for the PBC in the UK for the five administrations between 1951 and 1974. He finds that the myopic hypothesis never outperforms strategic hypotheses and in only two periods outperforms the naive, no change in unemployment hypothesis. Thus he finds little evidence of the manipulation of the unemployment suggested by MacRae's PBC model, but he does find support for the hypothesis that governments manage unemployment as if they are trying to maximise social welfare.

Frey (1978b and c) considers some evidence concerning political business cycles in the US and the UK in unemployment, inflation and growth of real disposable income. Tufte (1978) also presents, mainly anecdotal evidence supporting a PBC in real disposable income in the US and a number of other countries, and suggests that monetary policy might have been used to generate this cycle in the US. Luckett and Potts (1980) test the hypothesis, due to Tufte, that incumbent Presidents have used monetary policy to stimulate the economy prior to presidential elections and then put on the monetary brakes in the post-election period. They use evidence on the majority vote of the Federal Open Market Committee (FOMC) to show that the hypothesis, that emphasis given by the FOMC to reducing unemployment and stimulating growth is greater in the two years prior to an election than in the two years following an election, can be rejected. For further discussion of tests of the PBC theory and its underlying hypotheses the interested reader is referred to Whiteley (ed.) (1980) and Hibbs and Fassbender (eds) (1981), which contain a number of interesting articles.

With regard to the EBC, the works of Kydland and Prescott (1980, 1982) represent the most complete modelling of the theory. Their models do not rely on monetary surprises to generate shocks, instead they concentrate on fiscal and technological surprises. In their (1982) model the combination of technological shocks and fabrication lags, to represent persistence, allows them to explain both growth and the cycle (i.e. dynamic economic development) in a general equilibrium framework. They try to explain a smoothed output series for the US post-war data, which deviate significantly from a linear time trend, and find it to demonstrate approximately eight-year cycles. The major test of their cycle theory is to explain quantitatively the co-movements of the deviations of the various economic series from the smoothed series. In the model the specifications of preferences and technology are close to those used in many applied studies, which allows them to check the reasonableness of many parameter values. Also they select certain parameter values to ensure that the model steady-state values are close to the average values recorded in the US economy over the period under study. These restrictions reduce dramatically the number of free parameters to be estimated in order to explain the cyclical co-variances. There are in fact only seven free parameters, with the range of two of them being severely constrained *a priori*. The model is estimated under a number of assumed combinations of parameter values and shocks. It demonstrated a reasonably good fit and, with a couple of exceptions, the results were found to be surprisingly insensitive to the values of the parameters. They argue that the fact that the co-variations of the aggregate variables in the model are quite similar for broad ranges of many of the parameters suggests that, even though the parameters may differ across economies, the nature of the business cycle can be quite similar.

4.5 SUMMARY AND CONCLUSIONS

Most of the serious econometric testing relating to the PBC and EBC theories has been of their underlying hypotheses, i.e. of the REH and NRH, for the EBC, and of the policy reaction and popularity functions, for the PBC. Adequate testing of these underlying hypotheses would, however, appear to require the simultaneous estimation of the various key relationships within larger systems than those so far considered. This is especially true if we endow agents with rationally formed expectations and give the government an objective function, with other than purely welfare maximising attributes, to optimise subject to a set of economic constraints.

A PBC model would require careful modelling of both the economy and the polity and also of their interrelationships. The common approach of assuming that the government maximises a simple quadratic welfare function, with two arguments, subject to an economic constraint represented by a linear, adaptive expectations augmented, Phillips curve, and to a myopic electorate, would seem to be woefully inadequate. The general conclusions seem to be that the necessary conditions, as indicated by the influence of economic variables on popularity and the relationship between policy instruments and the economic variables that affect popularity, for the government to generate the cycle are there. This is provided that it is accepted that governments can use policy manipulation to influence real variables. The interesting question that remains to be answered is whether, given the above necessary conditions, a cycle would be induced by the government if the voters were endowed with rational expectations, rather than assumed to behave myopically.

With respect to the EBC theory, tests of the REH and NRH are probably less conclusive than those for the underlying relationships of the PBC theory discussed above. Econometric work with the original, monetary-shock-induced EBC models has not proceeded to a conclusion, but Kydland and Prescott have made some progress with fiscal and technological shock-induced EBC models. EBC models in general impute to the government little influence on the cycle beyond that of being the generator of monetary or fiscal shocks. A next major step in the development of EBC models should be the endogenisation of the government, perhaps by giving it an objective function, if they are to explain adequately the behaviour of western mixed economies. The step of endogenising the government seems to be implicitly required by the Lucas critique of policy analysis under rational expectations. It is difficult to see how Lucas's valid criticisms can be accounted for without giving the government an objective function, known by rational agents, which it attempts to maximise in a game theoretic formulation.

A broad conclusion can thus be drawn. There is some evidence supporting the hypothesis on which both the PBC and EBC theories are founded. But, because the theories are contradictory in their assumptions, especially regarding the capability of government policy for influencing real variables and the ability of agents to collect and process information efficiently, they cannot both hold true in their present form. A great deal of econometric work, therefore, needs to be done and it is a fair guess that the best attributes of the two theories will eventually be meshed in a game theoretic formulation with an endogenous government.

5 Some Conclusions Concerning Business Cycle Modelling

5.1 INTRODUCTION

In this chapter some conclusions will be drawn from the discussion of business cycle modelling in the previous chapters. Section 5.2 aims to draw some conclusions concerning the role of the linearity assumption in business cycle modelling. Section 5.3 will consider the relationship between cycle and growth theory. Finally, Section 5.4 will draw some conclusions concerning the treatment of the government in business cycle modelling.

5.2 THE ROLE OF THE LINEARITY ASSUMPTION

The linearity assumption in cycle modelling involves the use of linear models to represent the cycle and linear econometric techniques to estimate and test cycle models. The tendency has been to accept that linear models with stable solutions are adequate representations of the economy. This is evidenced by the econometric studies reported in Hickman (ed.) (1972), and is also accepted by the new classical economists (see Lucas and Sargent, 1978). The Frischian approach to modelling the business cycle has, therefore, been accepted by Keynesians and new classicists alike. The models reported in Hickman (ed.) (1972) in fact demonstrated so much stability, (i.e. monotonic rather than cyclical dampening) that autocorrelated shocks were usually required to generate realistic cycles in the simulation studies undertaken.

The major new modelling possibility, offered by the introduction of nonlinearity, is the limit cycle solution. This is a repeated cycle around an unstable equilibrium. If the limit cycle is stable then the cycle, and not the moving unstable equilibrium point tracing the (average) growth path, should be regarded as the natural dynamic motion of the economy. The cycle can, therefore, be regarded as the natural state of affairs and an endogenous (to the economic system) cycle theory could be developed. The role of shocks in such a system would be to impart the necessary irregularity to conform to real-world observations. It is also to be noted that limit cycles need not have symmetrical expansionary and contractionary phases, as sine waves do. Thus nonlinear theories can also account for the differences between the expansionary and contractionary phases of the cycle. In contrast, linear models offer only explosive, damped, or conservative cycle solutions, and monotonic explosive and damped solutions. The explosive solutions are of little use unless nonlinearities are introduced, such as Hicks (1950)-type ceilings and floors. Purely linear formulations, therefore, offer the choice between conservative and damped solution paths. The conservative solution may be ruled out, in the absence of nonlinearities, since in a stochastic formulation all of the energy is conserved and explosiveness is imparted. Thus, given that realism requires a stochastic formulation, choice is between the damped monotonic and damped cyclical solutions. It was noted that Frisch (1933) favoured the damped cyclical formulation as a solution to the propagation problem, with the cycle being driven by random shocks, which solve the impulse problem. Slutsky (1927) indicated that a model with a monotonically damped solution could generate a cycle if the shocks were autocorrelated, rather than random. It was noted that the Keynesian econometric models, reported in Hickman (ed.) (1972), tended to support the damped monotonic solution, autocorrelated shock formulation. Thus, in these models, the (moving) equilibrium is stable – there is a stable (trend) growth path along which the economy would progress in the absence of (autocorrelated) shocks. An adequate explanation of the impulse model that generates these autocorrelated shocks is clearly required, but is not provided, although Zarnowitz (1972) contains some discussion.

In an interesting paper, Blatt (1978) demonstrated the dangers of using linear econometric techniques in order to examine the business cycle which could be generated by a nonlinear system. Using a parameterised version of a Hicks-type nonlinear model Blatt generated some data. He then employed linear econometric techniques to find a best fitting model to explain these data. The estimated model fits well, and examination of the estimated parameters revealed that the data were generated by a stable system. Yet it was known that the data were in fact generated from a model with an explosive solution in which the explosiveness was contained by non-linearities, namely a ceiling and a floor.

What seems to be required, especially now that the economics profession has become increasingly familiar with developments in nonlinear mathematical and statistical techiques, is an analysis of the major economic relationships to check on their assumed linearity. Some suggestions for nonlinear function forms exist in the literature, e.g. for the investment and savings functions, and the Phillips curve. Other economic functions should, however, also be examined, because there is no certainty that economic systems are fundamentally linear, any more than physical or biological systems are.

5.3 BUSINESS CYCLES AND GROWTH

It was noted in the previous section that linear modelling, along Frischian lines, tends to lead naturally to the separation of cycle and growth theory: the cycle being due to, perhaps autocorrelated, shocks hitting an economy that would otherwise follow a stable equilibrium (natural) growth path. In the case of random shocks the cycle theory involves, essentially, the explanation of how these shocks are propogated into cycles, i.e. the explanation of persistence. In the autocorrelated shocks case, it is the modelling of the impulse generating mechanims that is perhaps the most crucial aspect of cycle theory. The explanation of the movement over time of the stable equilibrium point may be considered separately.

Nonlinear models, particularly those with stable limit cycle solutions, also tend to ignore growth. The equilibrium point, although unstable, is assumed to move over time and trace an (unstable) growth path. Its movement over time is usually treated as a feature requiring further discussion. There are, however, exceptions to this scenario in nonlinear modelling. Smithies (1957) and Minsky (1959) have used Duesenberry (1949)-type ratchet effects to explain both growth and the cycle in models based on multiplier—accelerator interaction. The Smithies model has been further analysed by Gandolfo (1980). Kaldor (1954) and Goodwin (1955) have argued that nonlinear modelling provides the opportunity to formulate a theory of dynamic economic development, capable of explaining both growth and cycles. Nevertheless, neither of these theorists, despite their major contributions to nonlinear cycle theory, provides a well-developed theory of dynamic economic development. Goodwin's (1951) contribution, for example, relies on exogenously generated technical change to explain trend growth. Kaldor acknowledges that changes in the capital stock may influence the cycle but does not link these changes to growth. Both Goodwin (1955) and Kaldor (1954) saw the linking of cycle and growth theory as potentially resulting from the further development of Schumpeter's work.

Schumpeter (1934, 1935) had argued that technical inventions occurred approximately continuously but that technological innovations occurred in bursts. The recession was a necessary part of the dynamic economic development because it created the conditions in which the built-in inertia of the economic system could be overcome by new enterprises and the introduction of new products and processes. Once the burst of development had started the process would culminate in a boom, then inertia would increase as the new enterprises become like the old enterprises and try to protect their market positions. A new recession is required to break this creeping inertia.

Marxist and Marxian economists have also viewed cycles and growth as part of the process of dynamic capitalism. Marx himself never presented a complete cycle theory, work in this area being on his list of work requiring future attention. He did, however, present a system explaining growth (expanded reproduction) and a number of suggestions for the cause of inter-ruptions in the process of expanded reproduction (crises). After a crisis a depression would follow and a process of readjustment, as in Schumpeter's work, would be necessary before expanded reproduction could resume. Marxist and Marxian literature has tended to concentrate on theories designed to explain these recurring crises. Such theories include the theories of over-investment, disproportionality, between the development of sectors, and underconsumption.[1] These main strands in the Marxist and Marxian literature have been influential in cycle literature in general.[2] The point of their argument is that, although expanded reproduction state is the main goal for the capitalist system and that it results in growth, due to the contradictions inherent in the system interruptions to the process of expanded reproduction occur and result in crises and cycles. Growth and cycles are thus inseparable in the capitalist system, the one creating the necessary conditions for the other. This is also, essentially, the view taken by Schumpeter (1934, 1935) and advocated by Kaldor (1954) and Goodwin (1955).

It seems difficult to escape the conclusion that a full theory of dynamic economic development, capable of explaining both the cycle and growth, and, perhaps, their interrelationships, is required. This is especially true if a nonlinear modelling strategy is adopted which explains the cycle endogenously, because such a theory should also explain the movement over time of the unstable equilibrium point around which the limit cycle occurs.

5.4 THE GOVERNMENT AND THE BUSINESS CYCLE

It was observed in Chapter 3 that the modern cycle theories, namely the modern PBC and EBC theories, are inconsistent in that they have very different views about the abilities of economic agents and voters to obtain and process the information relating to their decisions. The EBC models usually assume rational expectations formation, and costless information gathering and processing, so that expectations formation is equivalent to taking the mathematical expectation based on knowledge of the economic model conditional on all the available information. In contrast, the voters in modern PBC models are not assumed to be able to forecast the future effects of present economic policies, and are assumed to take more notice of recent, rather than past, economic performance in forming their evaluation of a government prior to voting. The electorate, therefore, behaves myopically and does not vote strategically, i.e. in the manner likely to secure the best long-run economic outcome. Clearly there is a case for introducing a weaker, but perhaps more economically rational, form of the REH and for examining its effects on the conclusions of these two modern theories of the cycle. The weak rational expectations formation hypothesis would acknowledge that agents and voters incur costs, in terms of time and effort at minimum, of collecting and processing information. They would, therefore, collect and process information to the point where the marginal cost from doing so would equal the marginal benefit from doing so. Under such circumstances the agents and voters would be unlikely to be endowed with knowledge of the workings of the true economic model. Consideration would have to be taken of the learning processes involved and of the disequilibrium dynamics involved in convergence to the rational expectations equilibrium.

Even in the weak rational expectations case the Lucas (1976) critique of policy analysis, discussed in Chapter 3, would be germane. Thus, even within the EBC framework, some account would have to be taken of the objectives of the government in choosing its policies, if the (weakly) rational agents are to form their expectations and adjust their behaviours in order to best achieve their own objectives. Hence, if we are to progress beyond Lucas's observation: that, at least major, policy changes will elicit responses by agents which will result in changes in the parameters of the model and render analytical and simulation policy analysis with, assumed, fixed parameters useless; a game theoretic formulation is required. This is because once a government, like all other economic agents, is acknowledged to have an objective function which it aims to maximise and the government is assumed to know that agents possess (economically) rational expectations forming procedures, the government will expect responses to its policy changes by the agents. Further, it will know that these responses will be based on knowledge of its own objectives and the pursuit, by the agents, of their own, perhaps conflicting, objectives. Additionally, the government knows that the agents know that this is the state of play and the agents know that the government knows that they know that this is the state of play. Once a game theoretic approach to policy analysis is adopted it is possible to analyse the method by which policy rules are chosen and what their effects will be under the (economically) rational expectations formation hypothesis. The endogenisation of the government, by giving it an objective function, is however required as a prerequisite to a game theoretic analysis.

The main role of the modern PBC theory is to suggest the arguments that would be expected to enter the government's objective function, if the government was assumed to have the capability of influencing real, as well as nominal, economic variables by its policy choice. The arguments, suggested by modern PBC theory, would be those economic variables that influenced government popularity and also those that related to the ideology of the government, such as the distribution of income which may, in turn, be related to inflation and unemployment.

An interesting question that remains to be tackled concerns whether the government, in attempting to maximise its utility or objective function subject to economic constraints and an (economically) rational, rather than a myopic, electorate, will generate a business cycle; or whether the cycle is in fact endogenous to the economic system in which the government and other economic agents are playing their games and trying to maximise their individual, and perhaps conflicting, utilities.

APPENDIX

A general linear deterministic second order differential equation may be written:

$$y_t'' + a_1 y_t' + a_2 y_t = b \qquad \text{A.1}$$

where y_t'' and y_t' are the first and second differentials of y_t; a_1, a_2 and b are constants, and the order of the equation is determined by the highest order of differential appearing in the equation. The term deterministic is used to denote the fact that no random error term appears in the equation.

If b is zero we have an homogeneous equation, and if b does not equal zero we have a non-homogeneous equation. Solution in the non-homogeneous case involves finding both a general (to the homogeneous equation) and a particular solution such that their sum is the complete solution. The general solution, denoted y_{ct}, involves finding a solution to the homogeneous form of equation (1), i.e. equation A.1 with b equal to zero imposed. The particular solution, denoted y_{pt}, involves finding an equilibrium solution such that $y'(t) = y''(t) = 0$, when b is allowed to take its true non-zero value. If b is in fact zero then no particular solution is required. Thus the y_{pt} component to the complete solution provides the equilibrium, or asymptotic, value of y and, concomitantly, y_{ct} reveals the deviation of y_t from equilibrium at time t.

It is to be noted that equation A.1 has a form in which y_t'' has a coefficient of one. If this is not the case the differential equation under consideration should be put into this form by dividing by

92

the coefficient on y_t''. The homogeneous form of equation A.1 is:

$$y_t'' + a_1 y_t' + a_2 y_t = 0 \qquad\qquad \text{A.2}$$

Solution proceeds using the trial solution $y_t = Ae^{rt}$, so that $y_t' = rAe^{rt}$ and $y_t'' = r^2 Ae^{rt}$. Hence equation A.2 becomes

$$Ae^{rt}\,(r^2 + a_1 r + a_2) = 0 \qquad\qquad \text{A.3}$$

If $Ae^{rt} \neq 0$ then this can be simplified to give:

$$r^2 + a_1 r + a_2 = 0 \qquad\qquad \text{A.4}$$

Equation A.4 is called the characteristic, or auxilliary, equation and the characteristic roots can be found using the formula for solving quadratic equations, so that:

$$r_1, r_2 = \frac{-a_1 \pm \sqrt{a_1^2 - 4a_2}}{2}$$

Thus the general solution to the homogeneous equation involves in fact two solutions: $y_{1_t} = A_1 e^{r_1 t}$ and $y_{2_t} = A_2 e^{r_2 t}$, where A_1 and A_2 are arbitrary constants. The general solution is found by taking the sum of these two solutions, so that $y_{ct} = y_{1_t} + y_{2_t}$.

Three cases are of interest: the distinct real root case (case 1); the repeated real root case (case 2); and the complex roots case (case 3). Case 1 occurs when $a_1^2 > 4a_2$; case 2 occurs when $a_1^2 = 4a_2$; and case 3 occurs when $a_1^2 < 4a_2$. In each case a definite solution is only found once values are given to A_1 and A_2. For this we require two initial conditions. These are values for y_t and y_t' when t=0, i.e. at the time origin. In case 1, with $r_1 \neq r_2$, the general solution is $y_{ct} = A_1 e^{r_1 t} + A_2 e^{r_2 t}$. In case 2, with $r_1 = r_2 = r$, $y_{ct} = A_1 e^{rt} = A_2 e^{rt} = (A_1 + A_2)e^{rt} = A_3 e^{rt}$, does not in fact give a viable solution, by $y_{ct} = A_4 t \cdot e^{rt} + A_3 e^{rt}$ does give a solution. Again two initial values, for y_t and y_t' at $t = 0$, are required to give a definite solution. Finally, case 3 yields a pair of conjugate complex (imaginary) roots: $r_1, r_2 = h \pm vi$, where i is the imaginary number $\sqrt{-1}$, $h = -a_1/2$, and $v = \sqrt{4a_2 - a_1^2}/2$. h is called the real part and v the imaginary part of each root. In this case $y_{ct} = A_5 e^{(h+vi)t} + A_6 e^{(h-vi)t} = e^{ht}(A_5 e^{vit} + A_6 e^{-vit})$. Again, two initial conditions are required to assign values to A_5 and A_6. Because $e^{vit} = \cos vt + i \sin vt$ and $e^{-vit} = \cos vt - i \sin vt$, it is clear that case 3 will yield a cyclical solution as a result of the dependence of the solution on a linear combination of sine and cosine waves. If we let $\alpha = A_5 + A_6$ and $\beta = (A_5 - A_6)i$, then $y_{ct} = e^{ht}(\alpha\cos vt + \beta\sin vt)$. The resulting cycles will be damped if $h < 0$, conservative if $h = 0$, and explosive if $h > 0$. If the solution was $(\alpha\cos vt + \beta\sin vt)$ a conservative cycle would result, with constant amplitude and duration, but the multiplicative term e^{ht} determines the degree of dampening. The cycle involved will be around y_{pt}. Cases 1 and 2 do not yield cyclical solution paths for y_t.

The analysis in the case of a second order linear deterministic differential equation is similar. The general form of the equation is:

$$y_{t+2} + a_1 y_{t+1} + a_2 y_t = c$$

where the order is determined by the largest time difference, a_1, a_2 and c are constants, and the equation has been transformed to assume that the coefficient on y_{t+2} is one.

The particular solution is found by trying a solution $y_t = k$ (a constant). Substituting into equation A.5 gives:

$$k + a_1 k + a_2 k = c \text{ and } k = c/(1 + a_1 + a_2)$$

$$\text{thus, if } (1 + a_1 + a_2) \neq 0,$$

$$y_{pt} = c/(1 + a_1 + a_2)$$

when $(1 + a_1 + a_2) = 0$, we look for a solution $y_t = kt$, and so on until a satisfactory solution is found, so that $y_t = kt^n$ with $n > 1$ may be required. Again y_{pt} represents an equilibrium, which may be a moving equilibrium if $y_t = kt^n$ ($n > 1$) is required.

The general solution to the homogeneous form is also required to give a complete solution. The homogeneous form of equation A.5 is:

$$y_{t+2} + a_1 y_{t+1} + a_2 y_t = 0 \qquad \text{A.6}$$

A trial solution of $y_t = Ab^t$ is then tried, so that $y_{t+1} = Ab^{t+1}$ and $y_{t+2} = Ab^{t+2}$. Substituting into equation A.6 gives, after factorising:

$$Ab^t(b^2 + a_1 b + a_2) = 0 \qquad \text{A.7}$$

assuming $Ab^t \neq 0$ gives

$$(b^2 + a_1 b + a_2) = 0 \qquad \text{A.8}$$

The characteristic roots (b_1, b_2) may then be found using the quadratic formula, and again three distinct cases result. In the distinct real roots case (case 1):

$$y_{ct} = A_1 b_1^t + A_2 b_2^t$$

In the repeated real roots case we use, for the same reason as for the second order differential equation,

$$y_{ct} = A_3 b^t + A_4 t b^t$$

In the complex roots case:

$$y_{ct} = A_5(h+vi)^t + A_6(h-vi)^t$$

De Moivre's theorem gives the result that

$$(h\pm vi)^t = D^t (\cos \theta t \pm i \sin \theta t)$$

where $D = h^2 + v^2$ and θ is such that

$$\cos \theta = h/D \text{ and } \sin \theta = v/D$$

Using this result we get:

$$\begin{aligned}
y_{ct} &= A_5 D^t (\cos \theta t + i \sin \theta t) + A_6 D^t (\cos \theta t - i \sin \theta t) \\
&= R^t[(A_5+A_6) \cos \theta t + (A_5-A_6)i \sin \theta t] \\
&= R^t[A_7 \cos \theta t + A_8 \sin \theta t]
\end{aligned}$$

where $A_7 = A_5 + A_6$ and $A_8 = A_5 - A_6$.

In each of the cases a complete solution is the sum of the particular solution and the general solution to the homogeneous equation, i.e. $y_{pt} + y_{ct}$, and the values of A_j are determined using initial conditions on y_t and y_{t+1}, to give a definite or exact solution to the particular case. Again y_{ct} determines the deviations from the equilibrium, given by y_{pt}.

Cyclical solutions will again result in the complex root case and the oscillations will be conservative if $D = 1$, explosive if $D > 1$ and damped if $D < 1$. Additionally, oscillations can result from negative real roots. In the second order case with two distinct real roots the long-run time path is determined by the dominant root, which is the root with the largest absolute value. The time path will be convergent if the dominant root is less than one in absolute value, and will be divergent if the dominant root is greater than one in absolute value. In the repeated roots case the time paths are also divergent or convergent according to whether the common root, b, is less than or greater than one in absolute value. Where all the real roots are positive no oscillations occur, but where there are negative real roots there will be oscillations.

NOTES

CHAPTER 1

1 National Bureau for Economic Research.
2 Cyclical solutions to difference and differential equations will be discussed in Chapter 2 and the Appendix.
3 See note 2 above.

CHAPTER 2

1 The model in fact accords to the assumptions of Hansen, Samuelson points out. For a more detailed discussion of multiplier—accelerator models and also for a discussion of inventory cycle models, see Mathews (1959).
2 See Goldberg (1961), for a discussion of how the solution paths of linear difference equations depend on the roots of the equation and on the relationships between the parameter values of the equations.
3 Readers unfamiliar with the mathematics of difference and differential equations should refer to the Appendix before reading this section.
4 The phase of a cycle essentially determines the position of the cycle in time, i.e. it determines the date at which each boom and slump occurs once the period of the cycle is determined.
5 If the dominant real root is greater than zero, any cycle will be around the path dominated by this root and the solution will not be stable, in cases where $n \geq 3$.
6 If the dominant real root is greater than one in absolute value, any cycle resulting from a complex root will be around the path dominated by this root and the solution will not be stable, in cases where $n \geq 3$.
7 See note 3 above.
8 i.e. data with the trend estimated and subtracted.
9 See Slutsky (1927) and Yule (1927).

10   Mandel (1980) argues, for example, that the capitalist economies have moved into the contractionary phase of a long (approximately 50-year) wave.

11   The data in Haavalmo's (1940) example is in fact generated by a second order autoregressive equation with a one period lagged random error term.

12   By a reasonable parameter value, in this context, is meant a value that is not inconsistent with conventional economic wisdom.

13   Kalecki envisaged the governments of future capitalist democracies pursuing successful anti-slump policies but encountering strong opposition from business leaders to any attempts to maintain the high employment level reached in booms. The fears that the workers would 'get out of hand' and the disadvantageous effects of price increases in the upswing on the *rentiers,* which make them 'boom tired', would lead them to put pressure on government departments. This pressure would induce the government to return to the orthodox policy of cutting the budget deficit and a slump would follow in which government spending would again come into its own.

14   National Bureau of Economic Research.

15   The natural rate of unemployment is defined by Friedman (1968, p. 8) as: 'The level that would be ground out by the Walrasian system of general equilibrium equations, provided there is embedded in them the actual structural characteristics of the labour and product markets, including imperfections, stochastic variability in demands and supplies, the cost of gathering information about job vacancies and labour availabilities, cost of mobility, etc.'

16   See Friedman (1974) for further discussion.

17   See Christ (1968), for example.

18   See Chrystal (1979, Ch. 9) for a useful review of the UK literature on crowding out; and Carlson and Spencer (1975) for a discussion of crowding-out pertaining to the US literature.

CHAPTER 3

1   See Muellbauer and Portes (1978 or 1979) for examples of some analysis typical of the disequilibrium approach.

2   See, for example, Branson (1979, Ch. 10, p. 204) for a discussion of this point.

3   The fabrication lags in the model arise out of the acknowledgement that multiple time periods are required to build new capital goods. The importance of these lags lies in the fact that only finished capital goods can be counted as part of the productive capital stock.

4   Some of the major references in the debate are: Kydland and Prescott (1977), Calvo (1978), Taylor (1979), Buiter (1980, 1981), Chow (1981) and Shiller (1978).

5   By strategic voting, MacRae (1977) means that the electorate communicates its preferences in the short run through voting behaviour, to ensure that

the party in power promotes the social good in the long run. The electorate must, therefore, learn how the party in power responds to its voting behaviour and then adapt its voting behaviour accordingly, to secure the long-run, socially-optimum economic outcome. This contrasts with myopic voting behaviour which ignores the implications of current voting behaviour for the future state of the economy. For a discussion of strategic voting in committees, see Black (1958).

6 Reference cycles are representations of historical cycles in aggregate economic activity based on one or more key economic series. A number of stages (nine) in the references cycles, derived by the NBER, are identified. The relationships between earnings, labour productivity, labour costs, prices and profits in these cycle stages is analysed by Hultgren (1965). Hultgren's data are used by Boddy and Crotty (1975) in their study.

7 See Gandolfo (1980) for further discussion of the solution to such problems.

8 This is common for optimal control problems concerning economic policy. See Theil (1968).

9 See Gandolfo (1980), for example.

10 e.g. Frey and Lau (1968), Frey and Garbers (1971), Frey and Schneider (1978a, b and c, 1981 a and b, 1982), Frey and Ramser (1976), and Schneider, Pommerehne and Frey (1981); see also Frey (1974).

11 See Tullock (1976) for further discussion of the MVT.

CHAPTER 4

1 The structural neutrality hypothesis (SNH) is related to the natural rate hypothesis (NRH). It postulates that fully anticipated changes in the money supply can have no lasting effects on real economic variables, which are to be explained by the interactions of the real economic forces that determine their long-run equilibrium, natural rates, and by the variables that explain their short-run, cyclical deviations from these natural rates.

2 Revankar (1980) and Hoffman and Schmidt (1981) discuss the nature of these restrictions in more detail. A problem of observational equivalence between Keynesian and monetary reduced form models could, however, arise, even under the REH. See Barro (1981, Ch. 2, pp. 62-7) for a useful discussion of the observational equivalence problem.

3 A nested testing procedure is one in which the hypotheses are ordered according to their restrictiveness and then tested by comparing a more restricted model with a less restricted one. Thus, in this case, the SN hypothesis can be tested by comparing the RESN restricted model with the RE restricted model, in a likelihood ratio test. This will provide a valid nested test of the SN hypothesis if the RE restrictions have already been accepted in a nested test of the RE restricted model against an unrestricted, by the RE restrictions, model. Further, the RE restrictions

can only be validly accepted if the unrestricted model's restrictions, e.g. restrictions implying the exclusion of certain economic variables from the model, have previously been accepted in a test of the unrestricted model against the unrestricted reduced form model. The latter is the model in which each of the endogenous variables are regressed on all of the exogenous variables in the model. It is clear from this discussion that the SNH cannot be tested without invoking a nested testing procedure. This is because the expected variables must first be eliminated, prior to the test for SN. The hypothesis underlying the expectations formation mechanism, used to eliminate the expected variables, must, therefore, be tested and accepted if the test for SN is to have any usefulness.

4 OLS = ordinary least squares.

5 i.e. $y'_{nt} = (1 - \beta L)^{-1} y_{nt}$ where y_{nt} is the natural rate of output at time t; see equation 3.7 and its derivation.

6 i.e. Koyck transformations could be employed. See Kmenta (1971, Ch. 11, pp. 474-9) for a discussion.

7 The process generating y_{nt}, used by Barro (1978), will not be duscussed in detail here, but it is worth noting that the extra variables, introduced through the process explaining y_{nt}, might solve the observational equivalence problem. See Barro (1981, Ch. 2, pp.62-7) for a discussion of the observational equivalence problem.

8 Δ is the first difference operator such that $\Delta x_t = x_t - x_{t-1}$. Some comment on the relevance of this assumption is germane. The reduced form supply hypothesis, discussed in Chapter 3, can be written:

$$y_{ct} = \alpha \sum_{i=0}^{\infty} \beta^i (m_{t-i} - m^*_{t-i}) + \sum_{i=0}^{\infty} \beta^i v_{t-i} \qquad 1$$

where $y_{ct} = y_t - y_{nt}$. This may be written, equivalently:

$$y_{ct} = \alpha \sum_{i=0}^{\infty} \beta^i (\Delta m_{t-i} - \Delta m^*_t - 1) + \sum_{i=0}^{\infty} \beta^i v_{t-i} \qquad 2$$

This is because $\Delta m_{t-i} - \Delta m^*_{t-i} = (m_{t-i} - m^*_{t-i}) - (m_{t-i-1} - m^*_{t-i-1})$ and under the rational expectations hypothesis, with expectations being formed using information up to period $t-1$, $m^*_{t-i-1} = m_{t-i-1}$, so that:

$$\Delta m_{t-i} - \Delta m^*_{t-i} = m_{t-i} - m^*_{t-i}$$

If, however, $DMR_t = \dfrac{\Delta M_t}{M_{t-1}} - (\dfrac{\Delta M_t}{M_{t-1}})*$, for example, was used to approximate discrete monetary growth, where M_t is the money supply at time t, rather than Δm_t, where $m_t = \log_e M_t$, then the specification (1) would differ from the specification (2). Thus the equivalence of (1) and (2) depends on the particular, $\log_e$ difference, representation of monetary growth employed by Barro.

9 See Barro (1978, p. 553) for a justification of the inclusion of the MIL_t variable.

10 i.e. a likelihood ratio test, in this case.

11 See note 3 above.

12 See note 8 above.

13 See Chapter 3 for a discussion of the electoral popularity cycle.
14 See Mosley (1976) for further discussion of the satisficing theory of economic policy.
15 See Friedman (1957) for further discussion of the permanent income hypothesis.
16 See Grossman (1974) for further discussion of the 'loops' around the Phillips curve.

CHAPTER 5

1 See Sweezy (1970, part 3), Mandel (1968, Ch. 11), and Kuhne (1979, part III) for discussions of Marxist and Marxian theories of crises and depressions and as useful sources of further references.
2 See Ichmura (1954) for an example of a discussion of the relationship between the Kaldor (1940), Hicks (1950), and Goodwin (1951) theories, and various under-saving, over-investment, under-consumption and disproportionality theories of the cycle.

References

Adelman, I. (1965), 'Long cycles: fact or artifact?', *American Economic Review*, June, pp. 444–63.

Adelman, I. and Adelman, F.L. (1959), 'Dynamic properties of the Klein—Goldberger model', *Econometrica*, **27(4)**, pp. 597–625. Reprinted in A. Zellner (ed.), *Readings in Economics Statistics and Econometrics*, New York: Little, Brown, 1968.

Akerman, J. (1944), *Ekonomiskteori*, **II**, Lund.

Akerman, J. (1946), *Ekonomiskt skeede och polistka förändringar*, Lund.

Akerman, J. (1947), 'Political economic cycles', *Kyklos*, Vol. 1, pp. 107–17.

Allen, R.G.D. (1965), *Mathematical Economics*, London: Macmillan, 2nd edn. (1st edn, (1956.)

Alt, J. (1979), *The Politics of Economic Decline*, Cambridge: Cambridge University Press.

Anderson, E.E. (1977), 'Further evidence on the Monte-Carlo cycle in business activity', *Economic Inquiry*, Vol.XV, April, pp. 269–76.

Arcelus, F. and Meltzer, A.H. (1975a), 'The effects of aggregate economic variables on Congressional elections', *American Political Science Review*, **69**, December, pp. 1232–9.

Arcelus, F. and Meltzer, A.H. (1975b), 'Aggregate economic variables and votes for Congress: a rejoinder', *American Political Science Review*, **69**, December, pp. 1266–9.

Attfield, C.L.F., Demery, D. and Duck, N.W. (1981a), 'A quarterly model of unanticipated monetary growth, output and the price level in the UK, 1963–1978', *Journal of Monetary Economics*, **8**, pp. 331–50.

Attfield, C.L.F., Demery, D. and Duck, N.W. (1981b), 'Unanticipated monetary growth, output, and the price level, UK 1946–1977', *European Economic Review*, **16**, No. 2/3, June/July, pp.367–85.

Barro, R.J. (1976), 'Rational expectations and the role of monetary policy', *Journal of Monetary Economics*, Vol. 2, No. 1, January, pp. 1–32. Reprinted in Barro, R.J. (1981), *Money Expectations and Business Cycles*, New York: Academic Press.

Barro, R.J. (1977), 'Unanticipated money growth and unemployment in the United States', *American Economic Review*, Vol.67, pp. 101–15. Reprinted in Lucas, R.E. and Sargent, T.J. (1981), *op. cit.*

Barro, R.J. (1978), 'Unanticipated money, output, and the price level in the United States', *Journal of Political Economy*, Vol. 86, August, pp. 549–80. Reprinted in Lucas, R.E. and Sargent, T.J. (1981), *op. cit.*

Barro, R.J. (1980), 'A capital market in an equilibrium business cycle model', *Econometrica*, Vol.48, No.6, September, pp.1393–417. Reprinted in Barro, R.J. (1981), *Money Expectations and Business Cycles*, New York: Academic Press.

Barro, R.J. (1981), 'The equilibrium approach to business cycles', Ch. 2, in R.J. Barro (1981), *Money, Expectations and Business Cycles: Essays in Macroeconomics*, New York: Academic Press.

Barro, R.J. and Rush, M. (1980), 'Unanticipated money and economic activity', in S. Fischer (ed.), *Rational Expectations and Economic Policy*, Chicago: NBER, pp.23–48.

Baumol, W.J. (1959), *Economic Dynamics*, New York: Macmillan. (3rd edn. 1970.)

Bellante, D., Morrell, S.O. and Zardkoohi, A. (1982), 'Unanticipated monetary growth, unemployment, output and the price level in the United Kingdom: 1946–1977', *Southern Economic Journal*, Vol.49, No.1, July, pp.62–76.

Black, D. (1958), *Theory of Committees and Elections*, Cambridge: Cambridge University Press.

Blatt, J.M. (1978), 'On the econometric approach to business cycle modelling', *Oxford Economic Papers*, Vol.30(2), July, pp. 292–300.

Boddy, R. and Crotty, J. (1975), 'Class conflict and macro-policy: the political business cycle', *Review of Radical Political Economics*, Vol. 7.

Borooah, V. and Van der Ploeg, R. (1982) 'The changing criteria of economic success: performance and popularity in British politics', *Manchester School*, pp.61–78.

Box, G.E.P. and Jenkins, G.M. (1971), *Time Series Analysis, Forecasting and Control*, San Francisco: Holden-Day, 2nd edn.

Branson, W. (1979), *Macroeconomic Theory and Policy*, New York: Harper & Row, 2nd edn.

Bronfenbrenner, M. (ed.) (1969), *Is the Business Cycle Obsolete?*, New York: Wiley, Interscience.

Buiter, W.H. (1980), 'The macroeconomics of Dr. Pangloss: a critical survey of the new classical macroeconomics', *Economic Journal*, **90**, March, pp.34–50.

Buiter, W.H. (1981), 'The superiority of contingent rules over fixed rules in models with rational expectations', *Economic Journal*, Vol. 92, September, pp.647–70.

Burns, A.F. and Mitchell, W.C. (1946), 'Measuring business cycles', New York: NBER, *Studies in Business Cycles No. 2*.

Calvo, G.A. (1978), 'On the time consistency of optimal policy in a monetary economy', *Econometrica*, Vol.46, No.6, November, pp.1411–28.

Carlson, K.M. and Spencer, R.W. (1975), 'Crowding out and its critics', *Federal Reserve Bank of St. Louis Monthly Review*, December.

Chang, W.W. and Smyth, D.J. (1970), 'The existence and persistence of cycles in a nonlinear model: Kaldor's 1940 model re-examined', *Review of Economic Studies*, **37**, January, pp.37–44.

Chappell, D. and Peel, D.A. (1979), 'On the political theory of the business cycle', *Economics Letters*, **2**, pp.327–32.

Chow, G.C. (1968), 'The acceleration principle and the nature of business cycles', *Quarterly Journal of Economics*, August, pp. 403–18.

Chow, G.C. (1975), *Analysis and Control of Dynamic Economic Systems*, New York: John Wiley.

Chow, G.C. (1981), *Economic Analysis by Control Methods*, New York: John Wiley.

Chow, G.C. and Levitan, R.E. (1969a), 'The nature of business cycles implicit in a linear economic model', *Oxford Economic Papers*, August, pp.504–17.

Chow, G.C. and Levitan, R.E. (1969b), 'Spectral properties of non-stationary systems of linear stochastic difference equations', *Journal of the American Statistical Association*, Vol. 64, June, pp.581–90.

Christ, C.F. (1968), 'A simple macro model with a government budget constraint', *Journal of Political Economy*, **76**, February, pp.55–67.

Chrystal, K.A. (1979), *Controversies in British Macroeconomics*, Oxford: Philip Allan.

Chrystal, A. and Alt, J. (1981a), 'Politico-economic models of British fiscal policy', Ch. 11 in D. Hibbs and H. Fassbender (eds), *Contemporary Political Economy*, North-Holland: Amsterdam and New York.

Chrystal, A. and Alt, J. (1981b), 'Some problems in formulating and testing a politico-economic model of the United Kingdom', *Economic Journal*, **91**, September, pp.730–6.

Coddington, E.A. and Levinson, N. (1955), *Theory of Ordinary Differential Equations*, New York: McGraw-Hill.

Desai, M. (1973), 'Growth cycles and inflation in a model of the class struggle', *Journal of Economic Theory*, **6**, pp.527–45.

Desai, M. (1975), 'The Phillips curve: a revisionist interpretation', *Economica*, Vol.42, February, pp.1–20.

Desai, M. and Shah, A. (1981), 'Growth cycles with induced technical change', *Economic Journal*, Vol.91, December, pp.1006–1010.

Dewald, W.G. and Johnson, H.G. (1963), 'An objective analysis of the objectives of American monetary policy, 1952–61', *Banking and Monetary Studies*, Homewood, Illinois: R.D. Irwon.

Downs, A. (1957), *An Economic Theory of Democracy*, New York: Harper.

Dresche, F. (1947), Chs IX and XI in Samuelson, P.A. (1947), *op. cit.*

Driscoll, M.J., Ford, J.L., Mullineux, A.W. and Sen, S. (1981a), 'A note on the testing of the rational expectations and structural neutrality hypotheses for the UK', unpublished mimeo.

Driscoll, M.J., and Mullineux, A.W. (1981b), 'A direct test of rational expectations and structural neutrality: UK 1952–1979', unpublished mimeo.

Driscoll, M.J., Ford, J.L., Mullineux, A.W. and Sen, S. (1983a), 'Money, output, rational expectations and neutrality: some econometric results for the UK', *Economica*, Vol. 50, August, pp. 259–268.

Driscoll M.J., Ford, J.L., Mullineux, A.W. and Sen, S. (1983b), 'Testing of the rational expectations and structural neutrality hypothesis' *Journal of Macroeconomics*, Vol. 6, No. 3, Summer.

Duesenberry, J. (1949), *Income, Saving and the Theory of Consumer Behaviour*, Cambridge: Mass. Harvard University Press.

Fair, R.C. (1978), 'The effects of economic events on votes for the President', *Review of Economic Statistics*, May, pp.159–73.

Feiwel, G.R. (1974), 'Reflection on Kalecki's theory of political business cycle', *Kyklos*, Vol.27, pp.21–48.

Fisher, D. (1968), 'The objectives of British monetary policy, 1951–1964', *Journal of Finance*, Vol. 23, pp.821–31.

Fisher, D. (1970), 'The instruments of monetary policy and the generalised trade-off function, 1955–1968', *The Manchester School*, Vol. 38, September, pp. 209–22.

Frey, B.S. (1974), 'The politico–economic system: a simulation model', *Kyklos*, Vol.27, Part 2, pp.227–54.

Frey, B.S. (1978a), *Modern Political Economy*, Oxford: Martin Robertson.

Frey, B.S. (1978b), 'Politico-economic models and cycles', *Journal of Public Economics*, pp.203–20.

Frey, B.S. (1978c), 'The political business cycle: theory and evidence', Ch.4 in *The Economics of Politics*, Institute of Economic Affairs Readings, **18**, London.

Frey, B.S. and Garbers, H. (1971), 'Politico-econometrics – on estimation in political economy', *Political Studies*, Vol.XIX, No. 3, pp.316–20.

Frey, B.S. and Lau, L.J. (1968), 'Towards a mathematical model of government behaviour', *Zeitschrift für nationaloVkonomie*, 28, pp.355–88.

Frey, B.S. and Ramser, H.J. (1976), 'The political business cycle: a comment', *Review of Economic Studies*, pp.553–5.

Frey, B.S. and Schneider, F. (1978a), 'A political economic model of the UK', *Economic Journal*, Vol.88, No. 350, June.

Frey, B.S. and Schneider, F. (1978b), 'An empricial study of politico-economic interaction in the US', *Review of Economics and Statistics*, No.2, Vol. LX, May, pp.174–83.

Frey, B.S. and Schneider, F. (1978c), 'An econometric model with an endogenous government sector', *Public Choice*, **33**.

Frey, B.S. and Schneider, F. (1981a), 'A politico-economic model of the UK: new estimates and predictions', *Economic Journal*, **91**, September, pp.737–40.

Frey, B.S. and Schneider, F. (1981b), 'Recent research on empirical politico-economic models', Ch. 2 in D.A. Hibbs and H. Fassbender, *Contemporary Political Economy*, Amsterdam and New York: North-Holland.

Frey, B.S. and Schneider, F. (1982), 'Corrigendum', *Economic Journal*, **92**, June, p.410 (to 'A politico-economic model of the UK: new estimates and predictions', *Economic Journal,* **91**, September, 1981, pp.737–40).

Friedlaender, A.F. (1973), 'Macro policy goals in the postwar period: a study in revealed preference', *Quarterly Journal of Economics,* **87**, pp. 25–43.

Friedman, M. (1957), *A Theory of the Consumption Function,* NBER, Princeton University Press; London: Oxford University Press.

Friedman, M. (1961), 'The lag effect in monetary policy', *Journal of Political Economy,* Vol.69, No. 5, October.

Friedman, M. (1968), 'The role of monetary policy', *American Economic Review,* Vol. 58, No.1, March, pp.1–17.

Friedman, M. (1971), 'A monetary theory of nominal income', *Journal of Political Economy,* Vol. 79, March/April, pp.323–37.

Friedman, M. (1974), 'The counter revolution in monetary policy', *Institute of Economic Affairs,* Paper 33.

Friedman, M. and Schwartz, A.J. (1963a), *A Monetary History of the United States: 1867–1960,* NBER Studies in Business Cycles, No. 12, Princeton, New Jersey: Princeton University Press.

Friedman, M. and Schwartz, A.J., (1963b), 'Money and business cycles', *Review of Economic Statistics,* 45, No.1, February.

Frisch, R. (1933), 'Propagation problems and impluse problems in dynamic economics', in *Essays in Honour of Gustav Cassel.* London: George Allen & Unwin. Reprinted in R.A. Gordon and L.R. Klein (1966), *Readings in the Business Cycle,* American Economics Association.

Gandolfo, G. (1980), *Economic Dynamics, Methods and Models,* Amsterdam and New York: North-Holland.

Goldberg, S. (1961), *Difference Equations,* London: John Wiley.

Goodhart, C.A.E. and Bhansali, R.J. (1970), 'Political economy', *Political Studies,* Vol. XVIII, No.1, pp.43–106.

Goodwin, R.M. (1951), 'The nonlinear accelerator and the persistence of business cycles', *Econometrica,* Vol.19, No.1, January, pp.1–17.

Goodwin, R.M. (1955), 'A model of cyclical growth', in Lundberg E. (ed.), *The Business Cycle in the Post War World,* London: Macmillan.

Goodwin, R.M. (1967), 'A growth cycle', in C.H. Feinstein (ed.), *Socialism, Capitalism and Economic Growth,* Cambridge: Cambridge University Press, pp.54–8.

Granger, C.W.J. (1969), 'Investigating causal relationships by econometric models and cross-spectral methods', *Econometrica,* 37, pp.424–38.

Grossman, H.I. (1974), 'The cyclical pattern of unemployment and wage inflation', *Economica,* Vol.41, November, pp.403–13.

Haavalmo, T. (1940), 'The inadequacy of testing dynamic thoery by comparing theoretical solutions and observed cycles', *Econometrica,* Vol.8, pp.312–21.

Hansen, A.A. (1941), *Fiscal Policy and Business Cycles,* New York: Norton.

Hansen, A.A. (1951), *Business Cycles and National Income,* New York: Norton. (Enlarged edn, 1964.)

Harberler, G. (1958), *Prosperity and Depression,* London: George Allen and Unwin. (5th edn, 1964).

Harrod, R.F. (1948), *Towards a Dynamic Economics*, London: Macmillan.

Hayek, F.A. (1933), *Monetary Theory and the Trade Cycle*, London: Jonathan Cape.

Hibbs, D.A. (1977), 'Political parties and macroeconomic policy', *American Political Science Review*, Vol.71, Nos.3–4, pp.1467–87.

Hibbs, D.A. and Fassbender, H. (eds) (1981), *Contemporary Political Economy: Studies in the interdependence of politics and economics*, in *Contributions to Economic Analysis*, No.135, Amsterdam and New York: North-Holland.

Hickman, B.G. (ed.) (1972), *Econometric Models of Cyclical Behaviour*, Vols. 1 and 2, NBER Studies in Income and Wealth No.3V, Princeton University Press.

Hicks, J.R. (1949), 'Mr Harrod's dynamic theory', *Economica*, Vol. XVI, May.

Hicks, J.R. (1950), *A Contribution to the Theory of the Trade Cycle*, Oxford: Oxford University Press.

Hoffman,D.L. and Schmidt, P. (1981), 'Testing the restrictions implied by the rational expectations hypothesis', *Journal of Monetary Economics*, 15, pp.265–87.

Hotelling, H. (1929), 'Stability in competition', *Economic Journal*, Vol. 39, March.

Howrey, E.P. (1968), 'A spectrum analysis of the long swing hypothesis', *International Economic Review*, Vol.9, No.2, June, pp.228–52.

Hultgren, T. (1965), *Costs, Prices and Profits: Their Cyclical Relations*, New York: NBER.

Ichmura, S. (1954), 'Towards a general nonlinear macrodynamic theory of economic fluctuations', Ch.8 in K. Kurihari (ed.), *Post Keynesian Economics*, New Jersey: Rutgers University Press.

Isard, W. (1942), 'A neglected cycle: the transport building cycle', *Review of Economic Statistics*, Vol.XXIV, No.4, pp.149–58.

Juglar, C. (1889), *Des Crises Commerciales*, Paris: Guillaumin, 2nd edn.

Kaldor, N. (1940), 'A model of the trade cycle', *Economic Journal*, Vol.50, March, pp.78–92

Kaldor, N. (1954), 'The relation of economic growth and cyclical fluctuations', *Economic Journal*, March.

Kalecki, M. (1943), 'Political aspects of full employment', *Political Quarterly*, Vol.14, pp.322–30.

Karni, E. (1980), 'A note on Lucas's equilibrium model of the business cycle', *Journal of Political Economy*, Vol. 88, No.6, pp.1231–8.

Keynes, J.M. (1936), *The General Theory of Employment, Interest and Money*, London: Macmillan.

Kitchen, J. (1923), 'Cycles and trends in economic factors', *Review of Economic Statistics*, pp.10–16.

Klein, L.R. and Preston, R.S. (1969), 'Stochastic nonlinear models', *Econometrica*, 37, pp.95–106.

Kmenta, J. (1971), *Elements of Econometrics*, New York: Macmillan.

Kondratieff, N.D. (1935), 'The long waves in economic life', *Review of*

Economic Statistics, November.

Kosobud, R.F. and O'Neill, W.D. (1972), 'Stochastic implications of orbital asymptotic stability of a nonlinear trade cycle model', *Econometrica,* Vol.40, No.1, January, pp.69–86.

Kramer, G.H. (1971), 'Short term fluctuations in US voting behavior, 1896–1964', *American Political Science Review,* 65, No. 1, March, pp.131–43.

Kuhne, K. (1979), 'Economics and Marxism', Vol.II *The Dynamics of the Marxian System,* London: Macmillan.

Kuznets, S.S. (1930), *Secular Movements in Production and Prices,* New York.

Kydland, F.E. and Prescott, E.C. (1977), 'Rules rather than discretion: inconsistency of optimal plans', *Journal of Political Economy,* Vol.85, pp.473–92.

Kydland, F.E. and Prescott, E.C. (1980), 'A competitive theory of fluctuations and the feasibility and desirability of stabilisation policy', Ch.5 in Fischer, S. (ed.), *Rational Expectations and Economic Policy,* Chicago: NBER.

Kydland, F.E. and Prescott, E.C. (1982), 'Time to build and aggregate fluctuations', *Econometrica,* Vol.50, No.6, November, pp.1345–70.

Lachler, U. (1978), 'The political business cycle: a complementary analysis', *Review of Economic Studies,* No.140, June, pp.369–75.

Lachler, U. (1982), 'On political business cycles with endogenous election dates', *Journal of Public Economics,* Vol.17, pp.111–117.

Leiderman, L. (1980), 'Macroeconometric testing of the rational expectations and structural neutrality hypotheses for the United States', *Journal of Monetary Economics,* 6,pp.69–82.

Lepper, S.J. (1974), 'Voting behaviour and aggregate policy targets', *Public Choice,* Vol.18, Summer, pp.67–81.

Lewis, W.A. and O'Leary, J.P. (1955), 'Secular swings in production and trade', *Manchester School,* Vol.XXIII, May, pp.113–52.

Lucas, R.E. (1973), 'Some international evidence on output–inflation trade-offs', *American Economic Review,* Vol.63, pp.326–34.

Lucas, R.E. (1975), 'An equilibrium model of the business cycle', *Journal of Political Economy,* Vol.83, No.6 pp.1113–44. Reprinted in Lucas, R.E. (1981), *Studies in Business Cycle Theory,* Oxford Basil Blackwell.

Lucas, R.E. (1976), 'Econometric evaluation: a critique', in K. Brunner and A.H. Meltzer (eds), *The Phillips Curve and Labour Markets,* Carnegie-Rochester Conference Series on Public Policy No.1, Amsterdam and New York: North-Holland. Reprinted in Lucas, R.E. (1981), *Studies in Business Cycle Theory,* Oxford: Basil Blackwell.

Lucas, R.E. (1977), 'Understanding business cycles', in K. Brunner and A.H. Meltzer (eds), *Stabilization of the Domestic and International Economy,* Carnegie-Rochester Series on Public Policy, Vol.5, Amsterdam and New York: North-Holland, pp.7–29. Reprinted in Lucas, R.E. (1981), *Studies in Business Cycle Theory,* Oxford: Basil Blackwell.

Lucas, R.E. and Rapping, L.A. (1969), 'Real wages, employment and inflation', *Journal of Political Economy*, pp.721-54.

Lucas, R.E. and Sargent, T.J. (1978), 'After Keynesian macroeconomics', in Federal Reserve Bank of Boston Conference Series No.19, *After the Phillips Curve: Persistence of High Inflation and Unemployment*. Reprinted in Lucas, R.E. and Sargent, T.J. (eds) (1981), *Rational Expectations and Econometric Practice*, London: George Allen & Unwin.

Luckett, D.G. and Potts, G.T. (1980), 'Monetary policy and partisan policies', *Journal of Money, Credit and Banking*, Vol.12, No.3, August, pp.540-6.

McCullum, B.T. (1978), 'The political business cycle: an empirical test', *Southern Economic Journal*, Vol.44, Part 3, pp.504-15.

McCulloch, J.H. (1975), 'The Monte-Carlo cycle in business activity', *Economic Inquiry*, Vol.13, No.3, September, pp.303-21.

McCulloch, J.H. (1977), 'The Monte-Carlo hypothesis: a reply', *Economic Inquiry*, Vol.XV, October, p.618.

MacRae, D. (1977), 'A political model of the business cycle', *Journal of Political Economy*, pp.239-63.

MacRae, D. (1981), 'On the political business cycle', Ch. 10 in D.A. Hibbs and H. Fassbender (eds), *Contemporary Political Economy*, Amsterdam and New York: North-Holland.

Mandel, E. (1968), *Marxist Economic Theory*, London: The Merlin Press.

Mandel, E. (1980), *Long Waves of Capitalist Development: The Marxist Interpretation*, Cambridge: Cambridge University Press.

Mann, H.B. and Wald, A. (1943), 'On the statistical treatment of linear stochastic difference equations', *Econometrica*, Vol.11, Nos. 3 and 4, July-October.

Marx, K. (1867), *Das Kapital*, Vol.I. See also Vol.II (1885) and Vol.III (1894).

Mathews, R.C.O. (1959), *The Trade Cycle*, Cambridge: Cambridge University Press.

Mathews, R.C.O. (1969), 'Postwar business cycles in the UK', in Bronfenbrenner M. (ed.), *Is the Business Cycle Obsolete?*, London: John Wiley.

Metzler, L.A. (1941), 'The nature and stability of inventory cycles', *Review of Economic Statistics*, August. Reprinted in R.A. Gordon and L.R. Klein (eds) (1966), *Readings in Business Cycles*, AEA Readings, London: George Allen & Unwin.

Miller, W.L. and Mackie, M. (1973), 'The electoral cycle and the asymmetry of government and opposition popularity: an alternative model of the relationship between economic conditions and political popularity', *Political Studies*, Vol.XXI, No. 3, pp.263-79.

Minford, P. and Peel, D. (1982), 'The political theory of the business cycle', *European Economic Review*, 17, pp.253-70.

Minsky, H.P. (1959), 'A linear model of cyclical growth', *Review of Economic Statistics*, Vol.XLI, May.

Mintz, I. (1969), *'Dating postwar business cycles'*, NBER Occasional Paper

107, New York.

Mosley, P. (1976), 'Towards a "satisficing" thoery of economic policy', *Economic Journal*, Vol.86, March, pp.59–72.

Mosley, P. (1978), 'Images of the "floating voter": or the "political business cycle revisited"', *Political Studies*, Vol.XXVI, No.3, pp.375–94.

Muellbauer, J. and Portes, R. (1978), 'Macroeconomic models with quantity rationing', *Economic Journal*, December.

Muellbauer, J. and Portes, R. (1979), 'Macroeconomics when markets do not clear', Ch.16 in W.H. Branson (1979), *Macroeconomic Theory and Policy*, 2nd edn, *op cit.*

Muth, J.F. (1961), 'Rational expectations and the theory of price movements' *Econometrica*, Vol.20, No.3, July, pp.315–35.

Nordhaus, W.D. (1975), 'The political business cycle', *Review of Economic Studies*, April, pp.169–90.

Okun, A.M. (1980), 'Rational expectations – with misperceptions as a theory of the business cycle', *Journal of Money, Credit and Banking*, Vol.12, pp.817–825.

Patinkin, D. (1965), *Money Interest and Prices*, New York: Harper & Row. (1st edn, 1956.)

Pesaran, M.H. (1982), 'A critique of the proposed test of the natural rate – rational expectations hypothesis', *Economic Journal*, Vol.92, September, pp.529–54.

Phelps, E.S. (ed.) (1972), *The Microfoundations of Employment Interest and Money*, London: Macmillan.

Phillips, A.W. (1958), 'The relationship between unemployment and the rate of change of money wage rates in the United Kingdom, 1861–1957', *Economica*, pp.283–99.

Pissarides, C.A. (1972), 'A model of British macroeconomic policy, 1955–1969', *Manchester School*, **40**, pp.245–59.

Pissarides, C.A. (1980), 'British government popularity and economic performance', *Economic Journal*, **90**, September, pp.569–81.

Reuber, G.L. (1964), 'The objectives of Canadian monetary policy, 1949–61: Empirical tradeoffs and the reaction function of the Authorities', *Journal of Political Economy*, Vol.72, April.

Revankar, N.S. (1980), 'Testing of the rational expectations hypothesis', *Econometrica*, Vol.48, No.6, September, pp.1347–63.

Rose, H. (1967), 'On the nonlinear thoery of the employment cycle', *Review of Economic Studies*, Vol. 34, pp. 138–52.

Rose, H. (1969), 'Real and monetary factors in the business cycle', *Journal of Money, Credit and Banking*, May, pp.138–52.

Samuelson, P.A. (1939), 'Interaction between the multiplier analysis and the principle of acceleration', *Review of Economics and Statistics*, Vol.XXXI, May, pp.75–8. Reprinted in M.G. Mueller (ed.), *Readings in Macroeconomics* (1969) London: Holt, Reinhart and Winston, and discussed in A.C. Chiang, *Fundamental Methods of Mathematical Economics* McGraw Hill. (2nd edn, 1974.)

Samuelson, P.A. (1947), *Foundations of Economic Analysis*, Cambridge, Mass: Harvard University Press.

Samuelson, P.A. (1965), 'Some notions on causality and teliology in economics', in D. Lerner (ed.), *Cause and Effect,* New York: The Free Press.

Samuelson, P.A. (1967), 'A universal cycle?', *Operations Research Verfahren,* Vol.3, pp.307–320.

Samuelson, P.A. (1971), 'Generalised predator — prey oscillations in ecological and economic equilibria', *Proceedings of the National Academy of Science, USA,* **68.**

Sargent, T.J. (1979), *Macroeconomic Theory,* New York: Academic Press.

Sargent, T.J. and Wallace, N. (1975), '"Rational" expectations, the optimal monetary instrument, and the optimal money supply rule', *Journal of Political Economy,* Vol.83, No.2, April, pp.241–54. Reprinted in R.E. Lucas and T.J. Sargent (1981), *op. cit.*

Sargent, T.J. and Wallace, N. (1976), 'Rational expectations and the theory of economic policy', *Journal of Monetary Economics,* Vol.2, No. 2, April, pp.169–83. Reprinted in R.E. Lucas and T.J. Sargent (1981), *op. cit.*

Savin, N.E. (1977), 'A test of Monte-Carlo hypothesis: comment', *Economic Inquiry,* Vol.XV, October, pp.613–17.

Schinasi, G.J. (1979), 'A nonlinear dynamic model of short run fluctuations', *Review of Economic Studies,* Vol. XLVIII, pp.649–56, 1981.

Schneider, F., Pommerehne, W.W. and Frey, B.S. (1981), 'Politico-economic interdependence in a direct democracy: the case of Switzerland', Ch. 13 in D.A. Hibbs and H. Fassbender (eds), *Contemporary Political Economy,* Amsterdam and New York: North-Holland.

Schumpeter, J.A. (1934), *The Thoery of Economic Development,* Oxford: Oxford University Press. (Reprinted, 1969.)

Schumpeter J.A. (1935), 'The analysis of economic change', *Review of Economic Statistics,* Vol.XVII, No. 4, May.

Schumpeter, J.A. (1939), *Business Cycles: A Theoretical, Historical and Statistical Analysis of the Capitalist Process.* New York: McGraw-Hill, 2 vols.

Shiller, R.J. (1978), 'Rational expectations and the dynamic structure of macroeconomic models: a critical review', *Journal of Monetary Economics,* 4, pp.1–44.

Sims, C.A. (1977), 'Exogeneity and causal ordering in macroeconomic models', in C.A. Sims (ed.), *New Methods in Business Cycle Research,* Federal Reserve Bank of Minneapolis.

Sims, C.A. (1980), 'Macroeconomics and reality', *Econometrica,* **48,** January, No.1.

Slutsky, E. (1927), 'The summation of random causes as the source of cyclic processes', *Econometrica,* Vol.5, Part 2, pp.105–46.

Smithies, A. (1957), 'Economic fluctuations and growth', *Econometrica,* Vol.XXV, January.

Stigler, G.J. (1973), 'General economic conditions and national elections', *American Economic Review,* Papers and Proceedings, pp.161–7. See also 'Discussion', pp.178–80, and 'Comments' by P. McCracken, pp.

168–71 and A. Okun, pp.172–7.

Sweezy, P.M. (1970), *The Theory of Capitalist Development*, New York and London: Monthly Review Press.

Taylor, J.B. (1979), 'Estimation and control of a macroeconomic model with rational expectations', *Econometrica*, 47, No.5, September, pp.1267–86.

Theil, H. (1968), *Optimal Decision Rules for Government and Industry*, Amsterdam and New York: North-Holland.

Tobin, J. (1970), 'Money and income: *post hoc ergo propter hoc?*', *Quarterly Journal of Economics*, Vol. 84, May, pp.301–17.

Tobin, J. (1980), 'Stabilization policy ten years after', *Brookings Papers on Economic Activity*, No.1, pp.19–71.

Tufte, E.R. (1974), 'The political manipulation of the economy: influence of the electoral cycle on macroeconomic performance and policy', Princeton University, mimeo.

Tufte, E.R. (1978), *Political Control of the Economy*, Princeton, New Jersey: Princeton University Press.

Tullock, G. (1976), 'The vote motive', *Hobart Paper No.9*, London: Institute of Economic Affairs.

Varian, H. (1979), 'Catastrophe theory and the business cycle', *Economic Inquiry*, Vol. XVII, January.

Wardwell, C. (1927), *An Investigation of Economic Data for Major Cycles*, Philadelphia.

Whiteley, P. (ed.) (1980), *Models of Political Economy*, Sage Modern Political Series Vol.4, London: Sage Publications.

Yule, G.V. (1927), 'On a method of investigating periodicity in disturbed series', *Trans. Royal Society*, London, Vol.226.

Zarnowitz, V. (ed.) (1972), *The Business Cycle Today*, National Bureau of Economic Research General Series No. 96, Columbia, Ohio: Columbia University Press.

Zarnowitz, V. (1972), 'The business cycle today: an introduction', in Zarnowitz, V. (ed.) (1972), *op. cit.*

Author Index

113

Subject Index